Life In The Upper Country

LIFE IN THE UPPER COUNTRY

The Diary of Evelyn E. Amos 1948-1957

by
Evelyn E. Amos

cold-drill books
Boise State University
Boise, Idaho 83725

Perfectbound Edition
ISBN 0-916272-43-5
Library of Congress
Catalog Card Number 89-81945

Artist's Edition
ISBN 0-916272-44-3
Library of Congress
Catalog Card Number 89-81946

Family History

My mother, Estella Ramey, grew up on the Kansas prairie in sod shanties, sometimes hiding from Indians. When she was old enough, she did all of the sewing for herself and nine brothers and sisters until she married and moved to northern California. Later, she and her husband traded their shingle mill for 80 acres (sight unseen) in the sagebrush hills north of Sweet, Idaho. She had known the Sweet family, for whom the little village of Sweet was named, when they had all lived in Kansas.

Soon after they moved to Sweet, her husband died, leaving her alone, a tiny woman less than five feet tall. In order to make a living she grew vegetables and took them by buggy into the mining camps far up into the timbered mountains.

In order to protect her springwater rights, she staked out 360 acres of adjoining land for a homestead. A little neighbor girl walked four miles to warn her that other neighbors to the north were planning to slip over to Boise ahead of her and file the claim. She saddled her horse and rode over the hills through mud, rain, and dark of night to get to Boise ahead of them. This legacy was one of the ranches on which we were to grow alfalfa and to pasture cattle.

My father, Charles Bean, was one of seven boys born to parents who had migrated to Ohio from Maine. He grew up to be a horticulturist, went to Iowa, then later to a farm near New Plymouth, Idaho. He had been married twice, but was a widower when he moved to a farm north of Sweet—he had heard that frost wouldn't get his fruit there. His farm adjoined Estella's and, you guessed it—they were married and I came along, the 13th child of my father and the first and only one of my mother.

So I grew up near Squaw Creek—riding in the hills to round up the milk cows, searching for turkey nests under cottonwood trees, hiking the hills alone with the dogs and jackrabbits, and going to the little, white, one-room school (for which my mother had donated land).

My husband's father, Joe Amos, had come to Idaho from Missouri and had married a pioneer girl, Ida Cantrall, who, when a baby, had been carried to Idaho in a wagon from the gold-rush country of California. They built a home on a farm in the Montour Valley, where Clark, the oldest of four children, was born and attended school.

Clark and I were in the same grade at Montour High School, and graduated during the Great Depression. Two years later, in 1934, we were married in Sweet.

We lived on several different ranches in southern Idaho, but times being so hard, Clark had to go to work in the timber industry—logging, sawmill, truck repair, electric shop, maintenance superintendent.

We were living in a logging camp in northern California when we decided to return to Squaw Creek in August of 1948.

By this time we had three sons: Artell John, age 11 (referred to as Johnny because that is what his father calls him); Daniel, age 9; and Jimmy, age 7.

We wanted them to grow up in the wholesome atmosphere of the country, where they could have room for pets of their own, ride horses, and learn about the beauty of the wild out-of-doors.

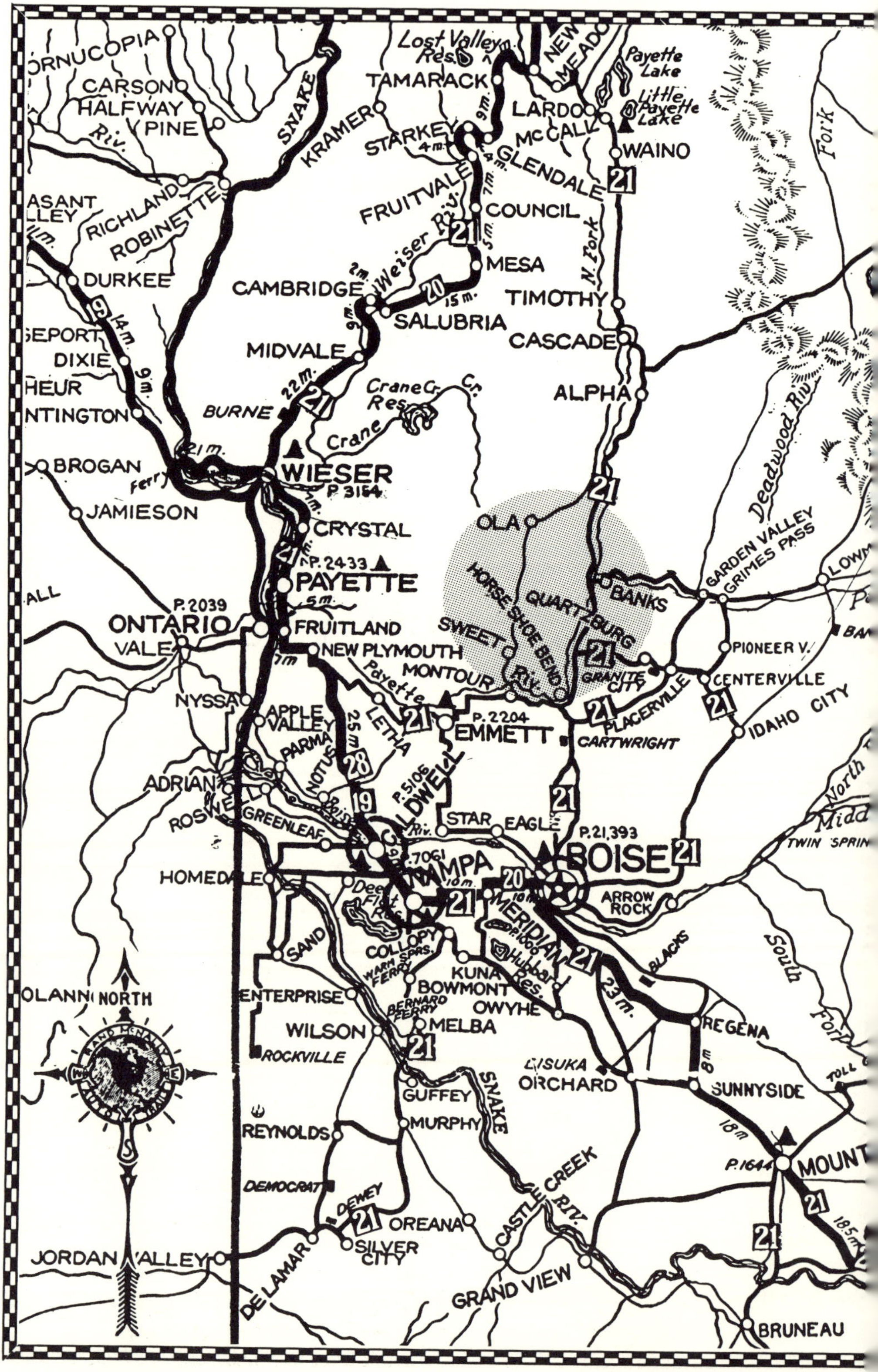

CORNUCOPIA
CARSON
HALFWAY
PINE
SNAKE
KRAMER
TAMARACK
Lost Valley Res.
NEW MEADOWS
Payette Lake
Little Payette Lake
LARDO
McCALL
WAINO
STARKEY
GLENDALE
FRUITVALE
COUNCIL
MESA
RICHLAND
ROBINETTE
DURKEE
CAMBRIDGE
SALUBRIA
TIMOTHY
CASCADE
MIDVALE
DIXIE
ALPHA
Crane Cr. Res.
BURNE
BROGAN
WIESER
P. 3154
JAMIESON
CRYSTAL
P. 2433
PAYETTE
OLA
HORSE SHOE BEND
QUARTZBURG
BANKS
GARDEN VALLEY
GRIMES PASS
Deadwood Riv.
ONTARIO
P. 2039
VALE
FRUITLAND
NEW PLYMOUTH
SWEET
MONTOUR
GRANITE CITY
PIONEER V.
CENTERVILLE
PLACERVILLE
IDAHO CITY
NYSSA
APPLE VALLEY
LETHA
EMMETT
P. 2204
CARTWRIGHT
PARMA
NOTUS
ADRIAN
ROSWELL
CALDWELL
P. 5106
STAR
EAGLE
P. 21,393
BOISE
GREENLEAF
NAMPA
P. 7061
HOMEDALE
MERIDIAN
ARROW ROCK
TWIN SPRINGS
SAND
COLLOPY
KUNA
BOWMONT
BLACKS
ENTERPRISE
OWYHE
WILSON
MELBA
REGENA
ROCKVILLE
ORCHARD
SUNNYSIDE
GUFFEY
REYNOLDS
MURPHY
SNAKE
P. 1644
DEMOCRAT
CASTLE CREEK
DEWEY
OREANA
JORDAN VALLEY
DE LAMAR
SILVER CITY
GRAND VIEW
BRUNEAU
NORTH

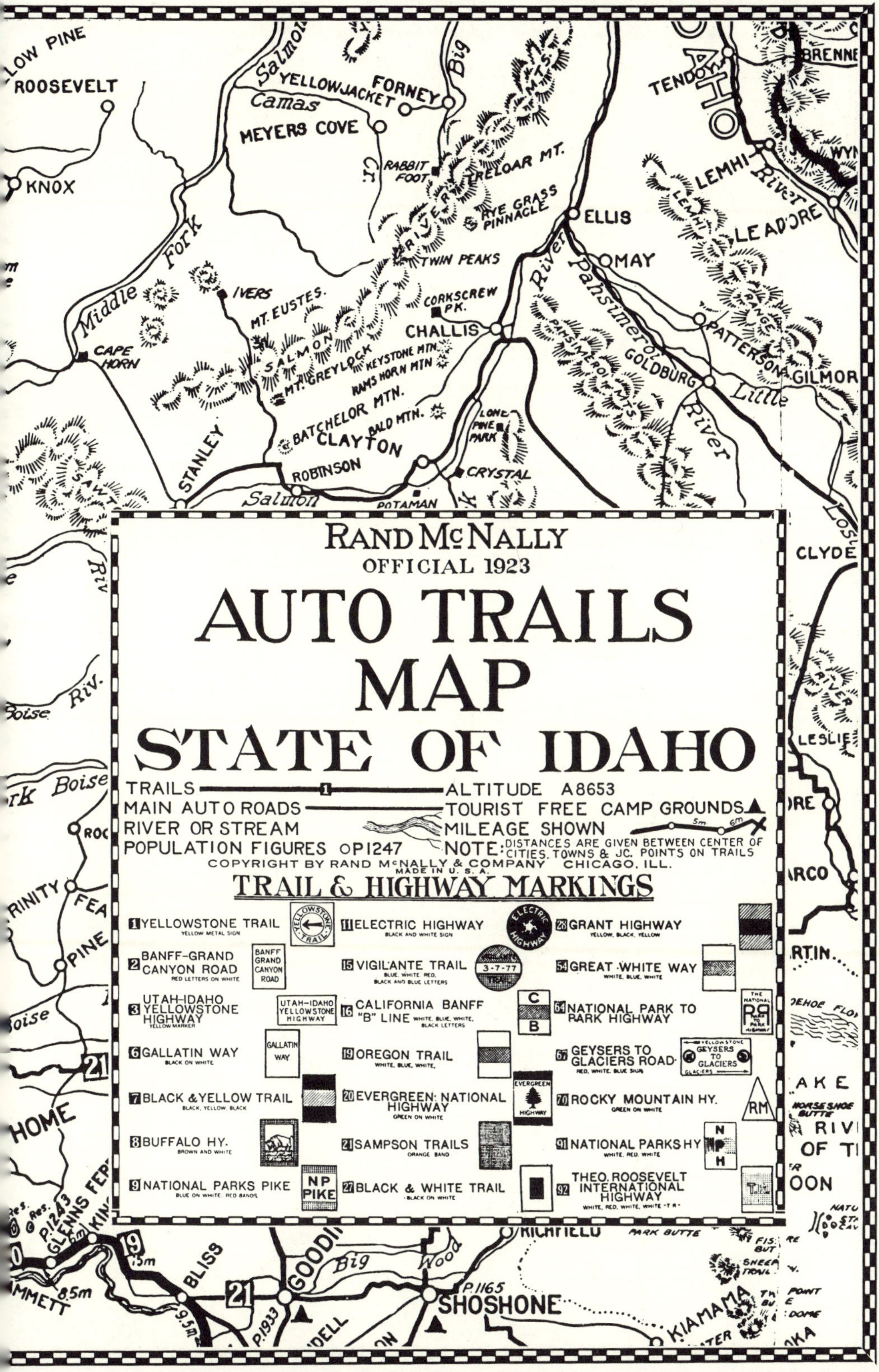

RAND McNALLY
OFFICIAL 1923
AUTO TRAILS MAP
STATE OF IDAHO
TRAILS
MAIN AUTO ROADS
RIVER OR STREAM
POPULATION FIGURES OP1247
ALTITUDE A8653
TOURIST FREE CAMP GROUNDS
MILEAGE SHOWN
NOTE: DISTANCES ARE GIVEN BETWEEN CENTER OF CITIES, TOWNS & JC. POINTS ON TRAILS
COPYRIGHT BY RAND McNALLY & COMPANY CHICAGO, ILL.
MADE IN U. S. A.
TRAIL & HIGHWAY MARKINGS
1 YELLOWSTONE TRAIL
YELLOW METAL SIGN
2 BANFF-GRAND CANYON ROAD
RED LETTERS ON WHITE
BANFF GRAND CANYON ROAD
3 UTAH-IDAHO YELLOWSTONE HIGHWAY
YELLOW MARKER
UTAH-IDAHO YELLOWSTONE HIGHWAY
6 GALLATIN WAY
BLACK ON WHITE
GALLATIN WAY
7 BLACK & YELLOW TRAIL
BLACK, YELLOW, BLACK
8 BUFFALO HY.
BROWN AND WHITE
9 NATIONAL PARKS PIKE
BLUE ON WHITE, RED BANDS
NP PIKE
11 ELECTRIC HIGHWAY
BLACK AND WHITE SIGN
ELECTRIC HIGHWAY
15 VIGILANTE TRAIL
BLUE, WHITE, RED, BLACK AND BLUE LETTERS
3-7-77
16 CALIFORNIA BANFF "B" LINE
WHITE, BLUE, WHITE, BLACK LETTERS
C
B
19 OREGON TRAIL
WHITE, BLUE, WHITE
20 EVERGREEN NATIONAL HIGHWAY
GREEN ON WHITE
EVERGREEN HIGHWAY
21 SAMPSON TRAILS
ORANGE BAND
27 BLACK & WHITE TRAIL
BLACK ON WHITE
28 GRANT HIGHWAY
YELLOW, BLACK, YELLOW
54 GREAT WHITE WAY
WHITE, BLUE, WHITE
64 NATIONAL PARK TO PARK HIGHWAY
67 GEYSERS TO GLACIERS ROAD
RED, WHITE, BLUE SIGN
GEYSERS TO GLACIERS
70 ROCKY MOUNTAIN HY.
GREEN ON WHITE
RM
91 NATIONAL PARKS HY
WHITE, RED, WHITE
N P H
92 THEO. ROOSEVELT INTERNATIONAL HIGHWAY
WHITE, RED, WHITE, WHITE "T R"
ROOSEVELT
KNOX
YELLOWJACKET
FORNEY
Camas
MEYERS COVE
RABBIT FOOT
TRELOAR MT.
RYE GRASS PINNACLE
ELLIS
TWIN PEAKS
MAY
IVERS
MT. EUSTES.
CORKSCREW PK.
CHALLIS
Middle Fork
CAPE HORN
SALMON
MT. GREYLOCK
KEYSTONE MTN
RAMS HORN MTN
BATCHELOR MTN.
BALD MTN.
CLAYTON
LONE PINE PARK
STANLEY
ROBINSON
CRYSTAL
Salmon
POTAMAN
TENDOY
LEMHI
LEADORE
PAHSIMEROI MTS.
Pahsimeroi River
PATTERSON
GOLDBURG
GILMOR
Little River
CLYDE
LESLIE
Boise Riv.
TRINITY
PINE
HOME
GLENNS FERRY
BLISS
GOODING
Big Wood
SHOSHONE
RICHFIELD
KIAMAMA
PARK BUTTE

— YEAR OF 1948 —
RETURNING

November 1 *Nomenclature*

This Canyon Ranch is what is commonly called a small dry-land cattle ranch, containing slightly over seven hundred acres of rocky, mountainous grazing land, except for sixty tillable acres which are scattered in fifteen different plots on both sides of Squaw Creek, for two-and-one-half miles. These are mostly little creek-bottom fields, some of them extending back on rises where the ground can be cultivated. Since in many places between the fields the mountains come down abruptly to the creek edge, there are no accessible locations on which to build wagon roads to connect them. Therefore, machinery has to be pulled back and forth across the creek—and this creek is no rivulet—it is rods wide and feet deep during high water.

In the earlier days this much land supported three families. Now, because the taxes, production, and living costs are so much higher, it isn't enough for one family.

At the southern end of the ranch there is an old house and barn built on a windy hill overlooking the winding creek and steep cliffs. We call this the Lower Place. At the northern end are located the buildings and house wherein we live. In between these two farmsteads and on the opposite side of the creek is an old, rock, house foundation and big black locust trees, built and planted by a pioneer family. This we refer to as the Middle Place. Six miles farther south, we have another four hundred acres known to be The Eighty.

November 30 *Gory*

This sad story begins before Thanksgiving Day when we borrowed a big, red, white-face boar from a neighbor.

One evening the hog had disappeared and we spent time off and on for four days searching the roadsides, the hills, the brushy ravines before we finally found him wandering along the highway halfway back to his home. We tried to drive and coax him into the stock trailer, but to no avail. By waving wicked looking sticks at him, we did at last persuade him to stroll ponderously back to our barnyard.

At dusk a few days later Johnny came running breathlessly to the house gasping, "Mama, get the flashlight and come quick!" For an instant my heart nearly stopped beating, as I feared that Clark had been cornered by the hog. Then he continued, "Daddy thinks the boar has killed old Baldy!"

We dashed out to find Clark coming from the pasture carrying a pitchfork and leading the saddle horse which was dripping blood and dragging one hind foot.

"Listen to that hog roar!" Clark called out. "I had to keep fighting him off with the pitchfork to keep him away from the horse."

A few minutes later Clark drove off to get the help and advice of a neighbor who is an expert with horses, and back in the barn by dim lantern light they bound the horse's leg to stop the bleeding.

Before he went home, the neighbor warned, "Don't go near that hog. Stay clear away from him. Once they go mad and get the taste of blood, they will attack anything!"

He needn't have warned me—coward that I am—I wouldn't even step from the door the following morning after a sleepless night. But Clark managed to climb up on top of the hog shelters and pour some grain down into a trough below; when the boar rushed in to greedily gobble it up, Clark quickly jumped down, slammed the heavy wooden panel shut, and locked him in. We all breathed easier! Two days later it took three men and a lot of lassoing and pulling and prodding to get the powerful beast loaded into the trailer. They cut off his two long vicious tusks and prepared him for market. Imagine! He had been a barnyard pet, ridden by children, at home; we had driven him with little sticks!

But the poor old saddle horse lay dead. It was then that we found holes in his abdomen where the sharp tusks had gored him. Evidently, the enraged hog had hit him before he suspected any harm, because he had had plenty of space in the pasture for running away. He had been a grand old quarter horse—so full of spirit and trained in the art of cutting and turning cattle. However, his death may have saved one of us from tragedy, either from the danger of his falling with one of us, since his legs were getting stiff from age and were causing him to stumble frequently when running, or from an unexpected attack on one of us by the boar. Neither was he a safe horse for children. The last time that I rode him, Clark jumped on behind the saddle to ride across the creek. I guess it made Baldy a little peeved, as he started "kicking up" when we reached the middle of the stream. I, lacking in buckaroo ability, could see myself falling off in that icy water. What a relief to reach the other side where I could safely dismount on the dry sand!

December 4 Apprehension

Winter is coming upon us early and finding us sorely unprepared. Our first snowfall of the season, which came the seventh of November, unusually early for this altitude, covered up at least six weeks of dry grass grazing for the cattle.

At first, Clark hauled hay up from the Lower Place in the trailer with the tractor, but now he can't pull it over the hills and through the snow without getting stuck. Perhaps he could make it with a wagon and team of horses, but then the horses would have to be kept in the barn and fed precious hay that could winter several head of cattle. The horses, if left out on the snowy hills, can rustle a living from tall grass and brush, where cattle would starve.

So today we did the obvious thing—drove the milk cows down to the hay. We followed in their trail behind them through the ten inches of soft snow. Hunting up wire and boards and posts from under the concealing snow, we erected a temporary corral to keep them by the old barn near the hay.

December 6 Prince

After Baldy was gone and we needed a horse to carry us across the creek, a neighbor offered to sell us a big old black horse that would be safe for the boys to ride and also a good pack horse. We were glad to get him, although I wasn't so sure when I rode him the nine miles home, for he shied at every snow ball left along the side of the road by the snow grader!

Each morning and evening Clark rides the mile to the Lower Place, feeds and waters the cows, strips the little bit of milk from them, pours it into a two and one-half gallon cream can, ties the can onto the saddle, and rides back home. We would discontinue milking them, except that we must have milk for the boys.

December 10 Trail Blazer

We have purchased some cottonseed meal and ground grain to

supplement the short supply of hay. Every morning Clark measures out a definite ration into a sack, ties it onto the saddle, and takes it to the twenty head of range cows that are wintering across the creek near the two small haystacks on the Middle Place. He shovels snow out of the wooden feed troughs before sprinkling in the grain mixture; then while the cattle are busily licking it out, he carries hay on a pitchfork from the stack and scatters it on the snow.

Crossing the icy creek with the saddle horse isn't easy. The wise old horse is wary of ice that breaks through in spots, or ice that forms ledges out from the banks, or ice of two layers with water sandwiched in between. A person never knows from one morning until the next just where the thin ice will be.

And horses hooves weren't meant to have traction on ice. This morning Clark came back to the house and said, "I can't get Prince across the ice. It's so slick this morning that his feet slip in all directions, and I'm afraid he might fall and break his legs."

For once I had an idea, "Why don't you take all of the ashes from both stoves and sprinkle a trail across the ice?" He decided to try it, and it worked—the ashes melted into the ice just enough to roughen the surface.

December 20 Reinforcement

The range cattle have been breaking through the fence into the hay stack, and wasting the hay by pulling it down and trampling it. This we couldn't afford to allow, so, in between feeding chores, Clark and I went down to build a better fence. First we had to obtain some barb wire by pulling it from an old fence that the C.C.C. boys had built around a game-feed preserve years ago. Since I am not schooled in the art of pulling rusty staples from posts in freezing weather while wearing bunglesome wool mittens, my job was mostly stumbling around in the snow-covered rocks, trying to roll up the barby, unmanageable wire.

It seemed that we would never get it into rolls so that we could carry it over to the hay stack. I tried to ride the horse back, but my toes and fingers ached too bad from the cold. Then came hours of unrolling wire, stretching it between the posts, stapling it in place, and putting in extra posts for braces.

December 23 Balkiness

If there is anything I dread, it is having to help pull a car to get it started. But everytime we go anywhere in this cold weather (which is about twice a month) it is the same story—no start. It is a good thing that the school finally secured a bus—we never could have delivered the boys to school on time.

Now it is so cold that the tractor won't start either. Clark cranked and cranked and cranked and cranked until nearly exhausted trying to start it. I felt so sorry for him, I said, "Let's just forget about the whole thing. What if the boys can't be in the Christmas program, it won't kill anybody!" But he kept right on cranking and I kept right on pulling the choke until it fired, at last. Then we hooked a chain to the car and pulled it up and down the road behind the tractor for another hour before it started. I thought my feet would freeze riding up on that open tractor in the icy wind. We were afraid to take the chance of stopping the motor on the car so we let it run until time to leave for the program.

— YEAR OF 1949 —
SEVERE WINTER

January 11 *In the Cool of the Morning*

We had received a card from the veterinarian stating that he would be here at 8:45 this morning to vaccinate the heifer calves for immunization from the disease of brucellosis.

It was dark and twenty-five degrees below zero when we got the boys up at 6:00 a.m. to help drive the nine yearling calves to the barn from their feeding pen by the chicken house. We put on all of the wraps we could find, pinned wool socks around our faces, and started out. Owing to the deep snow, the calves stayed in the trails, and there were enough of us to block all exit trails; so, fortunately, we had them locked in the barn within a few minutes. Even so, we felt nearly frozen before we could return to the warmth of the heater.

When the veterinarian arrived at 10:00 a.m., the thermometer registered twenty degrees below zero. The vaccine and filled needle froze up so quickly that they had to be carried to the house to thaw out; then, Clark lit his blow-torch and took it to the barn to throw flames on the vaccine and needle until the vaccinating was completed.

January 15 *Clues*

Snow, especially crusted snow with a thin film of new soft snow on top, is quite revealing of the wild life on the ranch. Jigsaw patterns are formed as the tracks of snowshoe rabbits, cottontails, coyotes, pheasants, quails, deer, juncos, meadow mice, and bobcats interlace and are swept here and there by the tail of a porcupine.

We find that the flickers, magpies, and English sparrows stay with us all winter. Sometimes a little hawk dives after a sparrow in the barn. At night we can hear the hoot owl from the thicket up on the mountain by the spring.

January 17 Morale?

If this cold weather would only let up! Clark has frozen his cheeks and spots on his legs while riding back and forth to milk the cows. It keeps us going all day to get the chores done. Frequently, in fact, about every fifteen minutes, in the early morning I run (and I mean *run,* brrrrr) out to the garage to see if the flare which is supposedly burning under the tractor motor for warming purposes is safely under control. As soon as Clark gets back with the milk, he starts the tractor and drives six miles to a neighbor's ranch for a trailer-load of straw—a miserable trip through the zero wind, and the number of times that he will get stuck in the snow with the tractor at the stack yard is unpredictable.

We pump and carry water down the slick trail to the nine weaner calves, carry water to our one old speckled hen, carry water four times a day (to keep it from freezing solid in the troughs) to the six pigs in the barn, and carry water to the two fattening shoats in the chicken house. The sows are sleeping in the only dry place, the hay barn, and eating snow for water!

No time to relax. Low on wood, this cold weather takes so much. I build a fire in the cook stove just twice a day to conserve fuel. Everything is brought into the house to keep it from freezing: horse bridle (Clark usually uses the bridle only when he has difficulty in getting the horse to cross the creek; otherwise, he uses the halter to avoid having a bit to freeze to the horse's mouth), lariat, two garbage buckets, dog bread, washing machine, wet gloves under the stove, overshoes, wet overalls and coats hanging everywhere, water buckets sitting around—*what* housekeeping!

January 18 Rickets

The little pigs in the barn completely bury themselves under their straw to try to keep warm while sleeping. They have been shut in out of the snow and sunshine for so long that they appear to have developed the rickets. Anyway, they squeal and fall over with paralytic fits.

The horses have given up trying to live out on the hills and have come to the barn for some straw. The saddle horse must have lice, because he rubs on everything he comes to, until patches of hair are all worn off. He even tries to lie down in the snow to roll—saddle, rider, and all! I have been dusting him with rotenone powder, but there is no improvement yet.

Every night for weeks, and sometimes all day, I have had to keep the kerosene lantern lit in the cellar to save the fruit and potatoes from freezing.

January 20 Rabbits

Although a few deer have been around the feed yard all winter, they have done little damage compared to the herds of snowshoe rabbits that are now eating on the haystack at nights. Rabbit trails converge upon it from all directions.

After dark, whenever I step from the kitchen door, I hear the wire netting around the yard go "zing" and know that a rabbit is taking off from nibbling at dry flower stalks within the yard fence.

Our neighbor lost all of seventeen baby pigs because of the extreme cold, and bobcats killed two of his goats.

January 25 Odoriferous

Since we started mixing a gallon of cod liver oil into their grain ration, the pigs are feeling better. The weather is too cold for us to mix it out of doors, so we have to bring it in the house to stir and spill around in a wash tub—fishy smelling mess!

February 2 Cold Sunshine

According to the records printed in the newspapers, January officially went out as the coldest month in the history of the weather bureau for this area—and the records date back to 1864. It was a January with the most amount of sunshine, the least number of days with measurable precipitation, the deepest penetration of frost.

Even yet, the thermometer registered four degrees below zero this morning. Under its deep covering of ice, the usual creek roar is silent. Hanging almost to the ground from the house eaves, the huge icicles resemble silver swords.

The sink trap has to be thawed out each morning, and the pump would also freeze if we didn't trip it every night.

February 3 Cold Dust

We gave up trying to cut more green thorn wood—replaced the old barrel heater with our big oil-burning stove. Since I was the smaller (boys at school), it was my inglorious, unenviable, honorable, but unescapable duty to crawl under the house and worm my way on my stomach through the cold, dry dirt to place the copper tubing for the oil stove over a plank and up through a hole which Clark had drilled in the floor. Thank goodness, it was too cold for snakes and black widow spiders!

I had hoped that we wouldn't ever have to use the oil heater again. Contrary to advertisements, the heat rolls right up to the ceiling, making no place to warm icy toes. It takes hours for a really chilled person to get warm, and the air in the house has a stale, oily odor. We have another job: shoveling a road through the snow in the yard for the oil delivery truck.

February 4 Blizzard

This morning the hills are invisible from the house, the snow is pouring, and the wind is piling it in high drifts. Yesterday's wash (I neglected to bring in last night) was wound on the line or dragging in the snow drifts. Clothes won't dry outside in such cold weather.

Clark is *really* rationing out the hay and straw now. He is beginning to worry how the horses will be fed if the straw runs out. Shoveling the cattle-feeding troughs out from under the snow drifts when the wind is blowing is an irksome chore for him, because they start filling with snow again before he can get them all shoveled out.

The rabbits on the haystack have thinned out, either scared away or killed. Perhaps they are being slaughtered by owls or bobcats as there were four dead ones by the stack this morning.

February 5 Avalanche

Fresh snow and new drifts hid all signs of the snow slide into which Clark rode when on his way down the mountain trail to feed the range cattle. When the horse started sliding and plunging down the steep incline, Clark jumped off but caught his overshoe buckle in the stirrup and landed in the deep snow on his head. Prince finally came to a standing position down on the creek. Since he couldn't go through the slide, Clark decided to try breaking a trail on down the creek over the snow-covered ice. This wasn't very satisfactory because the snow drifts hid the thinner ice over the current, letting the horse break through twice—lucky it wasn't in deep holes.

February 6 Mountain Climbers

Deciding that a trail would have to be broken above the slide around the mountain, Clark started out with the boys, the horse, the shovels. From the window, I watched them slowly and laboriously pushing their way over the rugged terrain until they dropped from sight on the other side. They reminded me of mountain scalers I have seen in picture shows.

Hours later when they returned, Clark said the new trail was too hard on both man and horse, and the next day he would have to break another one down the other side of the creek. All of that work for nothing?!

February 7 Snowbound

During the night our driveway was blocked with drifts from another windy snow storm. This was the first time that the school bus couldn't get through. The snow plows had more than they could manage, for they didn't arrive during the day.

At dusk a neighbor arrived from the upper valley with his caterpillar tractor and bulldozed snow four feet high on both sides of the driveway and down to the calf pen with his tractor blade. While he was eating supper with us, we heard of the predicaments of other ranchers who were also snowed in.

February 8 Snow Oh?

Much snow—heavy snow—dry snow—glistening snow—melting snow—sub-zero snow—white snow—feed-trough burying snow—shadowy snow—track-imprinted snow—piled snow—deep snow—pheasant-killing snow—cold snow—crusted snow—wet snow—clean snow—blowing snow—powdery snow—swirling snow—hard snow—soft snow—slippery snow—drifting snow—trail-filling snow—shoveled snow—plowed snow—solid snow—crystal-flaked snow—sticky snow—plenty snow—grass-covering snow—light snow—enough snow—and it looks like more snow!

February 9 My Day

As we were unusually short of hay this morning, I decided to ride down to the Lower Place and do the milking for Clark while he left early for a load of straw.

In places the snow had so completely hidden the trail by drifting that I couldn't see any print of it. But Prince never missed a step or turn. By walking along with the tip of his nose in the new snow, he could somehow scent the old, packed trail. In other older drifts where I could see the trail, I dismounted and tried to jump from one deep horse track to another, for I feared the horse might fall with me. Soon I decided that his four feet were far more sure-footed than my two; so I remounted, but kept my feet free of the stirrups, just in case!

I removed Prince's bridle to let him eat hay while I put the six cows into their stanchions, rationed out their grain, milked them, boosted the heavy can of milk up and tied it to the saddle, and pitched hay down into the outside feeders from the waning supply in the center of the old, leaky barn.

All in all, it took me three hours to make the trip. My next chore when I got back was to shovel the snow out of the heifer calves' feed troughs, feed the calves some cotton-cake pellets and grain, and then watch to see that the magpies didn't carry off the pellets before the calves could eat them. Then I carried warm water and warm mash to the six pigs in the barn. I blew the flame out of the cellar lantern and refilled it with kerosene, brought the old, yellow tom cat into the house for some milk, walked to the road to get the mail sack, and took warm water down to the brooder house to the old speckled hen. Surprise for me! Two eggs in the corner.

When Clark came with the straw, we ate a quick lunch before shoveling and shoveling and shoveling snow in order to get the tractor and straw into the barnyard. When he pulled the load down into the calf pen, he got stuck in the snow again. In despair, he finally unhooked the trailer and shoveled enough more to get the tractor alone back up the hill to the house.

It was four o'clock in the afternoon when we started for the Middle Place to feed the range cattle—I in the lead on the horse with the meal tied to the saddle—Clark wallowing along behind in the snow. When we arrived at the haystack the cows weren't in sight, so Clark said he would shovel out the troughs while I looked for the cattle down in the brush along the creek.

By this time the wind was fiercely blowing a wet, thick snow into my face. I pinned an old wool sock over my ears and mouth, but my cotton gloves were dripping wet and cold. The wind and snow stung my eyes until I could hardly see into the brush. I followed and followed the cattle tracks until I found the creatures away down at the Lower Place, where they were eating willow shoots as though they were starved. They didn't want to be driven back. Every time I herded them together and started them back, the big old bull would lead off toward another clump of willows. I couldn't ride the horse through all the deep drifts to head them off, and I was about ready to quit when Clark came walking over the hill to help me. After much lunging and yelling and prodding, we got them back to the stack at dark. Another inch of snow had to be shovelled out of the feed troughs.

I was so miserable by this time that Clark said, "Take the horse and go on back to the house. I'll come when I get the hay carried out." But I knew that in the stormy darkness with the trail drifting over, anyone might get lost; whereas, Prince could take us home without missing a step on the trail no matter how dark it was. So I took shelter in the lee of the horse and waited.

When we finally dragged back to the house at eight o'clock, we could wring water out of our clothes. The boys had completed all of the evening chores and were waiting for me to fix supper.

Then we could have dropped over! One of the dogs had her mouth full of porcupine quills, which meant a half hour of holding her down to pull out the quills with pliers by the light of the kerosene lamp.

End of a wintry day.

February 10 Harbingers

When we arose this morning, we found that rain had started in the night and a break had come in our cold weather. I shovelled the heavy snow off the cellar and enjoyed being out in the rain and thawing air.

I could hardly believe my eyes when I saw two yellow grosbeaks in the wild chokecherry trees . . . I wonder if it is a sure sign of spring or if they will have to turn around and go back southward for food.

February 11 Boom!

Water running on top of the ice in the creek makes it difficult to cross with the horse again. Now and then we hear the boom of a snow slide and later see where great chunks of heavy snow have fallen on top of each other, forming small glaciers.

February 14 Valentine's Day

False hopes, I guess. Night before last it was ten below zero, and last night another big blowing snow storm filled the driveway. The snow depth is nearly three feet.

I think of people living within furnace-warmed homes in Boise, who never dream that certain people within fifty miles are having such a struggle to get through the winter.

February 19 Glacial Panorama

The horses snorted and ran up the hill. Clark and I ran for higher ground, too, not for safety, as our buildings are built above creek and field level, but to get a better view of the roaring scene below.

Huge chunks of ice pushed and piled and ground against each other, along with logs and fence posts and brush, as they leaped and plunged and rolled around the bend. A vast amount of dammed-up water behind the ice floe raised the water and ice level ten feet, and, in trying to push around the ice, flooded fields on both sides.

Clark had just returned from feeding across the creek a few minutes before!

When the last of the big floes disappeared from view, we came back to the house to get the car and drive down the road a few miles to watch the mass of floating ice break out of the narrow, deep canyon gorge and stall behind a small diversion dam.

February 24 Walls of Ice

Smaller floes and lone pieces of ice and driftwood still float on the high muddy water. The cattle across the creek had to go without hay on the day following the break-up.

To our dismay, great cakes of ice left stranded by the main floe, some three feet in depth, formed disorderly walls four to six feet high along both banks of the creek. One small field on the Middle Place was completely covered with a four-foot layer of jumbled ice.

Clark chose the crossing that looked to be the most accessible on the far side; and, taking axe, bar, and pick, climbed over big cubes of ice to the creek edge and started breaking and prying and pushing pieces into the current. The cakes were heavy and wedged in between boulders, but he managed to clear a horse trail through to the water's edge without falling into the icy water more than twice.

When he mounted Prince and started for the opposite side, the horse fell on his nose in the water when he stepped from an underwater ledge of ice that hadn't been swept away! Prince regained his footing, Clark was icy wet again, but they proceeded on across and onto the far bank without too much more ice prying.

March 1 "Caw Caw"

The boys happily rush in to report the arrival of flocks of blackbirds and crows and ducks. I am watching the first bare spot appear on the sunny side of the mountain, with gladness and hope that spring is really coming.

March 6 Wild Onions

Now there are about as many bare spots on the hills as there are snow drifts. Yesterday, through Johnny's new field glasses, we watched seven deer grazing in a patch of wild onions on the eastern mountain. The boys have delighted in the smell of the first wild green onions springing up on the hill back of the barn. We are proud of our yearling heifers; though they wintered on straw, cotton-cake, and grain, they are in good shape. This morning they swam the high water to rejoin the range cows on the hills.

March 13 Horse Silhouettes

First, the snow on the hills reminded me of a great, pure-white stallion—then a zebra with the stripes formed from long, bare ridges—then a pinto with huge, white blotches—then a buckskin with white feet and blaze face (dry grass and unmelted snowdrifts)—and last of all, a rough, speckled dun.

Thus ends our coldest, prolonged winter in history.

March 15 *Evisceration*

While butchering day was being put off again and again during cold weather, the two shoats grew too fat. However, today, with the help of a neighbor (who also brought a hog to be butchered), Clark finally managed to get them slaughtered. They were scalded in a vat of hot water over an out-door fire, so that the loosened bristles could be scraped off with a knife. Although the men worked steadily all day, except for dinner time, they couldn't finish the job before a drenching spring rain hit them.

March 25 *Lardy*

Those big sides of pork hanging out in the milk house looked so appetizing! After a week of working with them, though, I have rather altered my opinion. Using the kitchen for a work shop, we trimmed all of the excess fat from the hams, shoulders, bacons, and sausage meat; then we skinned the pieces of fat and sliced them small enough to run through the meat grinder. Next came the hours and hours of frying and stirring the ground fat in pans on the hot stove to remove the tissues and moisture. When we strained it through cloth into tin buckets, we found that we had twelve gallons of lard to store in the cool cellar.

Hot grease saturated the air and dripped from everything onto everything, including pans, dish towels, potholders, smoking stove, table, linoleum—Greasy Me!

After we ground the forty pounds of sausage (and maybe you think it doesn't take a lot of elbow grease to turn that hand meat grinder), we put it into a big tub, mixed it with sausage seasoning spices and salt, and re-ran it through the grinder. Last (but not least in work) was the job of forming it into patties, frying it, packing it into quart jars, and processing it in the pressure cooker for safe keeping in the cellar.

As soon as the smooth-trimmed hams, shoulders, bacons, and hocks were carried out and packed into a big wooden barrel, we covered them with a cooled, briny solution, prepared by boiling together a mixture of salt, brown sugar, and water in a wash boiler.

Cleaning pig feet to boil and pickle in vinegar isn't any picnic; neither is cleaning the heads. By boiling parts of the heads, then seasoning, grinding, and recooking, we made a big pan of head cheese.

We decided to try out an old Pennsylvania-German recipe called "liver puddin'." Into a big kettle went parts of liver, hearts, tongue, head meat, ears, and tails! When these were cooked tender enough for the bones to be easily removed, we dipped them from the broth and ran them through the food grinder; this mess was then returned to the kettle of broth to be simmered down with salt and pepper. We kept adding more pepper—more salt—tasting—more pepper—more salt—tasting—until it finally passed the taste test. This delicacy? It turned out to be a liver-flavored, peppery meat sauce, easily stored in jars, to be used during the winter for quick sandwiches or late Sunday supper snacks.

April 1 *Cute Little Chicks*

I don't suppose anyone likes little, soft, downy, day-old chickens better than I. It is a joy feeding them and watching them grow, from the incubator to the laying house, and then it is a pleasure to hear contented hens singing and cackling around their nests. Don't let anyone tell you, though, that chicken raising is a snap. It takes a lot of knowledge, patience, and routine, as well as a liking for chickens, to be a successful grower.

In preparation for our little flock, we had to remove bushels of old manure from the brooder house before we could scrub the floor with lye water and tack tar paper on the inside walls to keep wind from whistling through the cracks. The leaky roof had to be renewed by removing and replacing the old boards and covering them with asphalt roofing paper. Inside, we set up a little coal-burning brooder stove, over which was an umbrella-shaped hover to hold the warmth close to the floor. Around the bottom edge of the hover, I hung a narrow fringe curtain made of burlap (for the little ones to duck under, like a mother hen's feathers). In the circle around the stove we set up an eighteen-inch-high wall, made from cardboard boxes, to hold the chicks close to the heat and out of the cold corners. We dumped feed on newspapers until the chicks could learn to distinguish feed from litter.

At last the room was dry and warm for the three-hundred Austra-whites (sturdy crosses from white Leghorn hens and big black Australorp cocks) when we brought them home from the hatchery. Gently we carried the three, flat, blue boxes of hungry peepers down into their house and, before putting them by the stove, dipped each chick's beak into a pan of warm water.

Within a few moments they were picking at the grain mash that we had sprinkled on the newspapers, and making little, contented "perts" that so characterize a satisfied chick from an uncomfortable "cheeping" chick. After the water fountains were placed conveniently for them and the stove refueled and regulated, we reluctantly left them.

The first night, I arose twice and went down with my flashlight to fix the fire in the brooder stove. The first time, the chicks were all stretched out sound asleep in a circle around the hover. I looked at the thermometer. Sure enough, the stove was too hot in spite of the thermostat, so I didn't dare refuel it. The next time that I went down, the fire was out, and the babies were cold and heaped in a pile under one side of the hover! Frantically, I began lifting them to the other side; luckily, I had found them before those on the bottom of the heap had smothered. The fire was started and regulated again. Wearily, I slipped back to bed.

April 15 Peach Smoke

The curing meat has been removed from the brine in the barrel and hung up on wires in the little "smoke house" which stands down the hill under a sweet cherry tree. We have to trot down there frequently to replenish the fuel on the small fire which we keep smoldering at the end of a tiny tunnel leading under the wall of the smoke house. Only certain kinds of wood can be used to make a smoke that will impart the correct, non-bitter flavor. We are using wood from peach trees. Smoke pours from every crack, stings my eyes, and scents my hair. But do those hams look and smell delicious, dripping with their smoke-browned flavor! Soon we will wrap them in heavy waxed paper and store them in a frozen food locker in town.

May 1 Black Feet

Every night for a whole month I have had to get up at least once each night to attend to the fire in the brooder stove. Now the chicks are well-feathered and run around outside during the day. It wasn't easy to coax them out. They are so easily spooked that the least dog bark or bird whistle startles them into running back to the safety of the hover.

I have had to switch from tiny feed troughs to larger ones and make several more trips a day with feed and water. It is now easy to distinguish the white-feathered roosters from the black-speckled pullets whose legs have turned black. We will soon put roosting boards in the brooder house for them to learn to use, and remove the stove and hover.

May 21 Continuity

What a beautiful day! The sky is so completely blue in between white floating clouds—not a bit of smoke, dust or haze. Hummingbirds are hovering over the sweet, white pea-blossoms of the locust trees. King birds are building a nest in the tip-top of the woodshed. The trees of the yard are adorned with bright flashes of goldfinch and oriole feathers streaking here and there—judging from the numbers of birds, this must be a bird utopia.

All over the yard, the wild butter-and-eggs are opening their two-lipped, yellow and orange spurs; on the hills, the flowers of the balsam root, whose bright yellow blended so perfectly with the bluish-gray of the sage on the steep slopes, is disappearing. I often wonder why the colors of nature blend beautifully, whereas man-made color arrangements frequently clash.

From the first mingled odor of buttercups, fresh grass, and dobey weed in the early spring, there is an uninterrupted succession of wild flowers throughout the summer until frost—crocuses, blue bells, pansies, yellow and blue violets, sego lilies, camas, sweet williams, nasturtiums, sunflowers, vetch, larkspur, loco-weed, wake robin, and many, many others that have miraculously managed to survive in the environment of the dry summer hills.

May 27 Syringa

Isn't it incredible that each kind of flower has an individual odor? Our Idaho State flower, the white syringa, is in full bloom. It is a wild, hardy, mock-orange shrub, growing from four to eight feet high along edges of creeks and ravines; from all directions, sweet scent from the waxy-petaled, white-laden branches fills the air.

Here in the yard the big orange poppies seem to be vying with the orioles for brightness of color. I was happy to get the house vines and low-hanging, bushy limbs of the elm trees pruned off. Before, when I looked out of the windows, it was like having scraggly, long hair hanging down over my face—now, suddenly having a short, neat haircut.

May 29 Coming . . . Coming

While Clark was fastening power wires on top of the wood shed, he discovered four little speckled eggs in the king birds' nest.

Yes, electricity is coming! We are so excited. Perhaps I'd better bake a cake! The electric power we have hoped and worked and talked and paid for, for so many months, will soon be here. The big pole and transformer look rather odd standing out there in the yard. Our line was surveyed and brought a mile over steep mountains, rough rocks, and the creek. Clark used our team of horses to skid the big poles over hills and gulches; now he is busy running wires and installing switches and outlets all over the farmstead.

June 2 *Ice Cream Coming Up!*

Press and Presto! The lights turn on! We carried the old kerosene lamps away to the cellar. The big refrigerator is merrily humming in the kitchen. My handy friends, the electric clock, iron, hair clippers, food mixer, sewing machine, waffle iron, and toaster have been unpacked at last. Standing beside the wood-burning cook stove, all in readiness for the hot summer meals, is my first electric range, a big, old-fashioned type with a handy, high oven. And how nice it is to "plug in" a quiet washing machine—with no sputtering, popping, stalling, oil-dripping, fumy gas motor to worry over.

July 1 *Good-Bye Peaches*

Our garden looks nice and is growing by leaps, but it is, of necessity, a late garden, because Clark had to remove old, dilapidated fences, hog pens, and cockleburs before he could start leveling the one and three-fourths acres of garden and pasture.

Under the instructions of the Soil Conservation engineers who did the surveying and staking for the leveling, Clark (using a small hand-trip fresno and team of horses to move the soil) cut a little rise here and filled a sunken place there, until all of the low and high spots were smoothed out into a slight gradual slope for irrigation.

Still we couldn't plant until we had shoveled and hauled loads of barnyard manure for fertilizer; plowed, harrowed, and smoothed the ground; and surrounded and divided it with barb and netting wire fence—one side to be the garden, the other to be planted to calf pasture, with a specially balanced mixture of grasses and covers (a seed formula worked out by agricultural experts). It all has a progressive look if you don't know about the dozen young peach trees that bore so heavily last fall. Regretfully, we had to pull them. The long, cold, winter weather killed every one of them, as well as a row of blackberries and some roses by the house.

August 3 *While the Sun Shines*

Haying is the biggest and longest job on the ranch. All hay-making equipment, teams, wagons, mowers, tractors, rakes, derricks, were gathered, put into working condition, and pooled with those of a neighbor's in preparation for the long, hot days and weeks of hard work ahead for men and boys, beginning when the alfalfa reached the full-bloom stage.

Around and around and around the fields, clipping layers of fragrant, green alfalfa plants (also a few legs from unfortunate pheasants that unwittingly nested beneath the foliage) with the sharp cutting blades of the mower. It sounds easy and fast, especially with a new tractor and mower, but where the hay was quite tall or thick, it kept binding on the sickle, so that the mower had to be continually stopped while someone pulled the pile of cut and matted alfalfa aside. After the hay had wilted for several hours, depending on weather and moisture content, the fellow with the hay rake and team of horses started around and around the same fields, his shirt tail flapping in the warm breeze as he raked and dumped the hay, first into rows, then into bunches. Next the two men and boys came with teams and wagons to haul the hay to the nearest stack yard. One boy rode on the wagon to drive and stop the horses near the shocks of hay and to replace the hay, which the men threw up onto the wagon with pitch forks, into a solid, well-balanced load.

By this time the hay with its mixture of cheat seeds and fire weeds was dry enough to sift out stickery, irritating dust, which was whipped up the workers' pants legs and down their sweaty collars by every movement of air. To the boys' tender, sensitive skins, it was slow, hot hours of misery; and if they thought there was the slightest chance of not being needed or missed for a few minutes, they would run for the creek, shake some of the chafing dust from their clothes, and take a dip in the cool water.

At the stack yard, one man loaded the big hay fork from the hay on the wagon; one of the boys drove derrick, pulling the loaded fork up over the stack by means of a horse, pole, pulley, and cable; the other man worked on the stack, dumping and placing the hay in the correct spots to build a straight, storm-resisting stack.

October 25 Berky Arrives

Ever since the boys joined the newly organized 4-H Club this spring, Johnny has been wanting something special for a project; hence, when our club team won the livestock judging contest and a trip to the Pacific Livestock Exposition in Portland, Oregon, we requested our club leader and the county agent to look for a Berkshire gilt.

The men managed to purchase three pigs (two for other club members), and a few days later we drove sixty-five miles to meet and greet and get the prize animals. On our way home we stopped at our county seat to unload the pig and have its picture taken with Johnny and the local merchant who is sponsoring this sixty-dollar project.

No, sir, this little purebred pig, whose name is Muller's Seventeen Second, out of Sire Epoch Pataha Improver and Dam Marchon Sixteen Second, has not left the show ring to become a nobody—her pug nose and sleek black lines are to be shown in the county newspaper!

December 28 Air Waves

Have you every been away from the sound of music for months? If not, you have no idea how wonderful it sounds, nor how much you miss it after you have been without it for so long. Even I, who in certain past days have been entirely sick of radio music playing all day long, can again bear to listen to the modern singers.

After electric power came to make a radio light up, we were too busy all summer to think much about not having one. This is not the first time that we have been without a radio, but it is the longest period that the children have experienced.

We decided to get a small radio for them for Christmas, to bring more cheer into the house until we can get our larger one repaired and find a place in our cramped quarters to set it. It is rather like visiting old friends again to hear Amos and Andy, Gene Autrey, and Charlie McCarthy.

Clark likes music best; of course, the boys like all the "crime busting" stories; and wouldn't you know? . . . round table discussions for me.

— YEAR OF 1950 —
FAIR DAYS

January 6 Following the Scent

This morning when I went down to feed the chickens, a white hen lay dead under the roost; blood on her neck provided circumstantial evidence of a visiting, nocturnal marauder. A faint odor of skunk clung to her feathers.

Since there were no open doors or windows, I began to wonder how a skunk could have entered. There were a few, little openings under the eaves which I decided to plug with pieces of burlap, and not knowing just how high a skunk might climb, I then clambered onto the roof to investigate. No woodpecker holes there, so I crawled back down and went back inside to have another look around. Suddenly I was startled to see a little head dodging around behind some nests. I took another quick look and made one big leap out through the doorway! What kind of a wild animal? Nothing but a tiny, black and white striped civet cat, more scared than I.

I hastened to the barn to find Clark and tried to hurry him into getting the twenty-two rifle; but for some reason, he didn't seem to be a very enthusiastic game hunter—kept wanting to know why I didn't get the gun and shoot the thing myself. After we finally prepared the rifle with ammunition and reached the hen house, we opened the door a trifle, then wider and wider when the civet cat seemed disinclined to jump at us. Cautiously, we peered all around before we spotted a bit of white wiggling hair behind a crack in a nest. Clark aimed at the crack and fired while I held the door open for his getaway!

Boy, what a strong atomizer for a small creature—fetid scent billowed from that coop like smoke. Clark was sick to his stomach and gagged all around the place, and neither of us could stand to re-enter the hen house for a couple of hours. When we did brave the offensive odor again, all we could see was the tail sticking out, which we eyed suspiciously as it seemed to move slightly. I waited another hour before going back to see if the tail still moved. When I opened the door, there, three feet in front of me, was little Mr. Polecat vainly trying to wriggle his full stomach though a small hole in the floor! I didn't dare hit him, with his automatic artillery pointing up toward me, so I stood there aghast until he finally squeezed through.

It didn't take me long to nail a patch over the hole which had evidently been concealed with litter when the hens started their morning scratching.

March 8 Amelioration

No more getting up at nights to stoke the brooder stove. With electricity comes the use of heat bulbs, with heat bulbs comes an easier way to start baby chicks. When they feel cool, they run under the heat light, which is cast from two bulbs hanging eighteen inches from the floor, and close their eyes for a little snooze while they are warming—in the same way that they might snuggle under a mother hen's feathers, if they had a mother hen. When they are warm again, they jump up, flap their little downy wings, and run for the feed and water. No more overheated air, no more dark nights of piling up to keep warm—for them it is supper time anytime.

April 28 Technicalities

When we decided to plant the fifty acres on the Eighty back to alfalfa (it has been used for growing grain so many years), we sought advice from farm magazines, pamphlets, neighbors, seed companies, soil conservationists, and the county agent, who took us on a tour of the most modern, dry land, alfalfa fields.

Here are some of the facts we gathered: Ranger alfalfa is one of the best of the newer varieties, taking less seed per acre, growing faster, and producing greater tonnage of hay; foundation is better than first, second, or third generations of certified seed when producing seed for sale; this seed is scarce and costs one dollar and twenty-five cents per pound; one and one-half to two pounds should be planted on each acre; if grown to produce seed, it should be planted in rows so that weeds can be controlled with a cultivator; these rows must run horizontally around the hills to prevent soil erosion and hold the moisture; the seeds should be planted in rows three feet apart, with a drill dropping the seeds one inch apart and two inches deep, three rows at a time; before planting, the ground must be plowed and then harrowed over and over until the clods are pulverized; immediately following the seeding, the soil must be packed down firmly with a heavy, rolling cultipack; and last, but by no means the least, PRAY FOR RAIN!

All of this advice Clark followed (but we must admit, not to the perfect letter) and, in time, with the help of a kind neighbor, completed the undertaking.

May 4 Wild Bees

While gathering wild "Woolly Breeches" for greens up on the hill by the springs, I noticed innumerable beetles and wild bees and flying ants and butterflies on the full, white blossoms of the thorn trees. Surely, blossoms growing on these hills should not lack for insect life to insure their perfect pollinization. Yellow goldfinches were scooping aphids off the thorn leaves with the sides of their bills.

This evening, as I stepped out to the side of the house, the rich odor of old-fashioned blue iris was near, trying to push aside the sweet scent of blossoming buck brush drifting down on the fresh air from the hills. The old yellow cat rubbed my legs and stretched out in the grass, his ears pointing in the direction of the night bird calling from the dark thickets along the creek. I wondered what kind of a bird it was—I never hear it in the daytime—and if old Tommy had any thoughts about a tender bird supper.

May 26 Last Day of School

Happy day around this predominantly masculine household!

All the families of the community, twenty-five more or less, gather in the school yard for favorite athletic contests in high jumps, broad jumps, foot races, three-legged races, relay races, potato sack races, vaulting. Then at noon everyone enters the school house and fills his plate as he files past the big, long tables loaded with huge white, chocolate, and angel cakes; potato, macaroni, and jello salads; meat sandwiches; potato chips; sweet and dill pickles; olives; pork and beans, and baked beans; hot chicken with noodles, and fried chicken; radishes; deviled eggs; berry pies; cottage cheese; cold fruit ade; hot coffee; and ice cream.

After all this has been stowed away, the dads stand the boys in a baseball game, while the mothers visit, pack up the bowls, and cheer the ball players. At last, everyone climbs into a loaded car and waves good-bye for the long summer vacation, which usually involves as much work as play.

May 28 Water Lift

The boys found out what picks were made for when they and Clark picked and shoveled, picked and shoveled dirt and rocks to form a new ditch around the hill below the barn to carry the big stream of water from our new, electric motorized, irrigation pump.

No more annoyance with the meager stream pumped by the old, balky gasoline engine. Now I can climb up onto the wooden platform which holds the pump and motor, open up the water faucet from the self-priming barrel, turn on the switch, and abruptly, water from a six-inch pipe rises several feet from the creek and pours out into our new ditch to run down over the pasture and garden.

My only regret about the new system is that it does not carry water high enough to irrigate a lawn by the house.

July 5 Feathers Mark the Spot

Early this morning when I went out to feed the thirteen broilers, and they didn't come running as usual to meet me, I had a sickening feeling that they were gone. When I opened the larger brooder house door, I found three badly roughed up and scared chickens hiding in a corner. A search through the weeds revealed three more bitten ones still alive, feathers and pieces of the others scattered all around.

Before we left on a picnic yesterday, we had shut the two dogs in the woodshed, but when we returned in the evening, they came to meet us—the woodshed door wide open, by what method we knew not. For some odd reason, the old collie always wants to chase chickens when we are gone. Perhaps that is his only chance. And, of course, when the big half-Chesapeake Bay retriever starts helping, with his bird dog instinct, and no one here to stop him, there is no limit until the chickens are all gone or have disappeared.

This isn't the first time it has happened, but it is the biggest loss. One day when we were away, with the dogs shut up, a pullet that had her nest in the woodshed found her way in through a hole in the window, and the dogs ate her!

July 20 Oleoresin Capsicum

When one of the boys came in to report that the little, red calf was bloating, we hastily hunted up the bottle of bloat medicine, mixed it according to directions, and poured it into a old beer bottle. Then Clark and the boys went down to the pasture to administer the relief.

This was a scraggly calf that Clark had bought at the sale for thirty dollars, and when he brought it home the boys had exclaimed, "Gosh, thirty dollars for that?" The first trouble with her was that she wouldn't drink milk, and when she ate too much green grass it bloated her. Then mange or some such skin disease began to take the hair from around her eyes and neck. After I mixed an oily preparation and doped her, Clark said, "You'll kill her for sure, putting that kind of stuff on her head!" So, sadly, I gave up, not wanted to be accused of wasting thirty dollars.

Suddenly I heard Clark yelling, "Water! Water! Bring some water. Quick, water!" Not knowing what the water urgency was for, I tried to think quickly whether to pump a glassful or a bucketful, but decided a quart can full, with a rag in it, might save the calf. I met Johnny at the fence where he grabbed the can and relayed it on. Thinking they wouldn't need any extra help, I went back to the house.

Soon Clark came hurrying in, wet, and rubbing his eyes. "Read on the bottle and see what's in that stuff! My eyes burn like fire!"

"Gracious!" I became alarmed as I reached for the bloat medicine bottle. "How in the world did you get it in your eyes?"

"The calf gave a big belch and the stuff blew out of her mouth, right into my face."

With my back turned, I started reading, "Cresol, oleoresin capsicum, oil of camphor, salicylic acid, turpentine . . ." on the label, when Danny came staggering in, looking like a drowned kitten. "Good night!" I exclaimed, "Where have you been?"

With a sheepish little grin, he said, "She blew it on me, too. I was standing beside daddy, but it burnt my eyes so bad that I started running toward the creek and felt my way over the fence and down over the rocks to the water. When I got there, I just ducked my head clear under!"

We decided that the salicylic acid, whatever that is, must be the irritating agent. After several more washings and eye ointmentings, their eyes were soothed enough that we decided perhaps I wouldn't have to rush them to the doctor, after all.

August 3 Evening Song

Along the creek the choke cherries are hanging in dark, ripe, heavy clusters. The nights are cool—just right to sit out and enjoy the song of the crickets, and to look down over the squash vines that are growing higher and higher, the tomato vines that are already waist high, and the bush beans which are so tall that they are falling over with weight—such a contrast to the over-dry hills where the wild sunflowers are struggling to bloom.

August 6 Y'all Come

If you want a frustrating job, just try finding men for a threshing crew. Every rancher is far behind with his own farm work, or working short-handed because there are no farm laborers to hire, or having his own grain combined and therefore doesn't need to exchange work, or just plain doesn't want to come in contact with grain dust on a hot day, and finds plenty of excuses for not coming. If men visitors from town drive in, they soon find that they have picked the wrong day, for they are handed a change of old clothes and a pitch fork or a shovel and put to work! But it is odd—no woman has ever come to help me with the potato peeling, pie baking, or stacks of dirty dishes!

By driving all over the valley, Clark finally managed to find a crew, then on threshing day some of them failed to come. But, in some hard way, the day's threshing was completed—505 bushels of barley from ten acres, heaped in the granary.

August 10 Cinema

We very seldom go to see a show; but, when we do decide to go, usually on the spur of the moment, there is a mighty rush to get the evening chores done. Going and coming twenty-five miles each way consumes nearly as much time as the show. If the evening is cool, we enjoy the ride through the little valley, down along the river road, across the rich bench land, and down again into the larger valley and town.

The boys see and distinguish between all the "makes" of cars on the road, admiring the late models, laughing at the rickety jalopies; while, I must admit, I know almost no model from another!

Clark admires the big, neatly-built stacks of fresh hay, the long green rows of corn, the ripening grain fields, the new silos. I enjoy seeing the cool lawns and flowers in front of the prosperous-appearing farm homes; the gorgeous sunset (the pleasure of which we are denied on the ranch, because the high, western hills hide the low horizon); the acres of peach, prune, pear, and apple trees that are beginning to ripen fruit; water spraying into the air from field sprinkler systems, which looks so cool and refreshing that I almost wish to stop and run over under the falling showers.

Clark and the boys discuss the merits of all the new farm machinery they see parked in the fields. All of us observe with pleasure the little, big-eyed, brown jerseys looking so docile and contented grazing in green clover pastures; and the big, black and white holsteins (we wish we had some like them) walking away from dairy barns. Most of the white-faced Herefords are in the mountains at this time of the year, but we do see one group of beef cattle—sleek, fat, black Angus.

Coming home after the show, we quickly leave the few neon lights, cross the river bridge, and climb the hill onto the bench land, from where we can see the stars shining above the outline of the encircling sage hills, and the slow flash of far off airplane beacon lights. Some of the farm living rooms are glowing with soft lights from reading lamps, others are dark at this early night hour. Soon we reach the big diversion and power dam with its many lighted posts gleaming in streaks on the quiet water. We wind on around the lake road where the rising moon shines on the ripples, and sharp mountain peaks across the river cast dark shadows far out onto the dark water. The fragrance of new-mown hay in the little valley is suddenly exchanged for that of dusty sage as we climb the hills back again to the ranch.

August 17 Fair Days

I wonder if our city cousins guess at the work their country cousins go through in order to show livestock at the fair.

All this show business was new to us; but, since exhibiting was part of Johnny's 4-H project, several days prior to the fair, he locked up in a clean, strawy pen three pigs from the fine litter that Berky had raised for him. He washed all of the mud from their hides; brushed their black, stiff hair until it shone; tried to teach them to walk in certain directions by the touch of a cane.

Excitement ran high on the day that the trailer was backed up to the barn door to load the pigs. Other 4-H children in the club kept waving and honking their car horns as they drove by with their loads of calves and pigs. Johnny was filling his wooden chest with pig grooming articles such as brush, currycomb, clippers, detergent; Clark was figuring what kind of a water trough and how many pounds of grain to take along; I was assembling and rolling up bedding and extra clothes. The paraphernalia at last all loaded, we hurriedly changed into clean, cotton clothes, and were off to the fair.

When we drove into the county fair grounds and found room to back the trailer into the doorway of the new, livestock exhibition building, it was one of the hottest afternoons of the summer. Exhibitors-to-be, old and young, with all of the help they could get from friends and parents, were hurrying in all directions—claiming stalls and printing and tacking up identification signs, setting up panels, unloading livestock, carrying buckets of water, leading calves in and out, scattering straw for bedding, brushing and belatedly clipping animals; while onlookers tried to keep out of the way of unruly steers and ferocious-looking dairy bulls being led with chains.

Some of the club boys were planning to sleep in the backs of trucks, some in an open tent frame, and others inside the building on small board lofts over the stalls. After we decided that we had helped Johnny all we could, we reluctantly left him, wondering if he would get any sleep that night amid all of the din, and started homeward to do the evening chores.

We returned to the fair a couple of times during the three days and found our boy doing all right, though how he could, on four hours of sleep each night and a diet of hot dogs and hamburgers, we didn't know. He had won some blue ribbons and prize money and was ready to go to Boise to the Western Idaho State Fair, so, again we loaded the pigs and hauled them on to Boise without returning them home.

Even more reluctantly, we left our son at the larger fair grounds, with few friends and no older person to look out for him. How could he stand six more days of heat and dust and flies and noise and catsup and mustard, without a rest and bath? Some of the 4-H boys and girls, on their own for the first time, squandered all of their money on carnival tricks and rides and soda pops the first day and had to beg money for food until their parents returned. We didn't worry about Johnny being so foolish with his money, but there was always the chance that he might lose it or have some pickpocket or rowdy take it from him.

However, nothing disastrous happened, and he managed to feed and groom and show his pigs and win enough ribbons in 4-H and open classes to pay his expenses.

I suppose the experience was good for him—he gained considerable knowledge in showmanship, and then, too, the cowboys taught him how to slip into the night rodeos without a ticket!

August 30 Pine Poles

The boys are learning how to make fence the hard way, from the ground up, or should I say, from the timber down. Early each morning they leave with Clark for the woods twenty miles away, where they cut small, six-inch in diameter lodgepole pines which Clark had purchased in the National Forest.

Clark fells the trees with the axe; the boys chop off the green, needle-covered branches, measure the trees either into post or pole lengths, and saw them accordingly. Then comes the toil of dragging them, one by one, and stacking them into piles close by a wood-road, where late in the afternoon they must be lifted, loaded, and tied onto the truck and trailer and hauled home over the narrow mountain road.

Since bark doesn't slip off easily on trees cut at this season of the year, it has to be sliced by hand from one end of the posts by pulling a sharp draw-knife under it. Then, in order to form points for driving into the ground, the barkless ends are sharpened by pushing them slantwise into a buzz saw—something similar to sharpening a pencil with a pocket knife, only on a larger scale.

The last process, before driving the posts into the ground, is to set the pointed ends into a solution of diesel oil and pentachlorophenol in an iron barrel from twelve to twenty-four hours, after they have been seasoned to remove the moisture content. This chemical treatment is rather expensive in the beginning, but experts at the agriculture experiment stations have found that treated posts withstand rot and insects up to fifteen years longer than untreated posts.

We have already used one-thousand posts. They are now cutting another thousand; Clark thinks it will take five-hundred posts a year to get our many miles of fences back into good shape and maintain them.

September 25 Daffy Derrick Driver

Luckily, nothing was crushed under it, the haystack, that is—there it lay, a big grain haystack sprawled out over the ground.

"I can get a neighbor to help restack it, if you will drive the derrick," Clark ventured. "It will be real easy. You can use the tractor and won't even have to walk or handle the cable."

"I'm afraid I'll do something wrong," I answered.

"Oh, it's so easy you couldn't possibly hurt anything."

So, reluctantly, I agreed to do my best. The next day we hooked the cable to the tractor; I pushed it into gear and started moving ahead to pull up the first big forkful of hay. All at once I heard a crackling noise and looked back. The men were waving and yelling. Suddenly I thought of the brake and clutch—perhaps I had better stop! When I looked again, the derrick base was rocking and the big boom pole falling, and both men were dodging and running to save their lives! As soon as my knees felt strong enough, I climbed off the tractor and learned that the cable pulley had broken, the rollers had flown in all directions, the chain had come loose letting the pole drop, and I had stopped just in time to avoid upsetting the derrick. (At least that is the way I understood it.)

In due time everything was re-assembled and the work continued satisfactorily. One last item: How does a derrick driver sit in constant readiness for the next pull without letting her mind wander to the creek or hills or the supper menu—and without having to be alerted with shouts?

November 1 Pigs or Rabbits?

We decided that those pigs across the creek would have to be caught before high water came. The old sow had hidden over there in the thicket to farrow her pigs. Now they were six weeks old and she had never brought them across when she came to eat her grain. Clark set up some temporary wooden panels to corral them in, and taking some burlap sacks in which to carry them back, we rode the horse across the water. The five of us took up positions around the acre of thorn thicket and started closing in.

Soon, amid the sound of running feet and threshing brush, came the shouts, "Head em off, they're going that way!" "Look out! They're coming toward the creek!" "Now they're scattering out and heading for the hill!" "There they come back again!" "I can't get around them! There they go!" After an hour of catching our hair and clothes in the thorn bushes, stepping in boggy pools, and running ourselves ridiculous, we gave up and sat exhausted. Those eight little spotted pigs could slip under the bushes and race up over the hill like jack-rabbits.

November 20 Come Home

First snow of the season today, and what do you suppose we found at the barn? Eight little spotted pigs! The old sow brought them over the water, and the funny part of it is—they don't act a bit wild, just eat at the grain troughs as though they had been raised there.

November 30 Pole Corral

The poles were work to cut and to haul from the woods, and heavy to boost up into place for nailing; the spikes are expensive and require a lot of elbow grease to drive through the thick wood; but when the corral is finished, it will be sturdy, horse and hog holding, and save us countless hours of running cattle around to catch or separate for this or that.

December 15 Hot Massage

When Clark went into the barn to milk this morning, he found old Nig's calf on its back in the manure trough. It was half frozen with its neck twisted around to one side; and, though it couldn't stand up, it could still breathe, so Clark carried it to the house and laid it on the floor beside the heater. Then, while he finished the milking, I rubbed the new-born calf's wet, black hair all over with burlap sacks, and held a heat lamp in position to finish the drying and warming process.

When, after a couple of hours, we stood it on its feet and it could balance alone, Clark carried it back to the barn to get some warm breakfast from its mother. Saved!

— YEAR OF 1951 —
HOT WATER

February 4 Corn Popper

Since Jimmy received an old-fashioned, long-handled popcorn popper for Christmas, he is the official popper at our house.

He has learned just how much corn, salt, and shortening to pour into the pan, and, when the first kernel jumps, to turn the electric burner off to maintain the proper heat without scorching until all of the kernels are popped.

Tonight we have the radio turned off so that Johnny can study at the kitchen table. The only sounds are the snapping of pine wood in the heating stove, the crunching of apples and buttered popcorn, the turning page of a magazine, the sliding lead of our pencils, snow blowing softly against the south windows.

February 25 It's So Peaceful!

About a week after New Year's Day, when snow came and cattle feeding started, the tractor up and got an ornery streak and wouldn't start except by cranking; and cranking made it more peeved than ever, so it gave a mighty kick which bent the crank and cracked the bone in Clark's wrist.

The hay rack on the wagon was broken and, since Clark couldn't harness the team with a bad wrist anyway, the tractor with trailer had to be kept at the Middle Place for further use. The catch to this is: it takes two people to feed with that outfit. "You know who" had to accompany Clark each morning for six weeks.

Until the creek was entirely frozen over, we broke the icy edges each morning so that we could ride Prince across the water; then we tied him to a tree and took to the treacherous, icy trail by foot. Get a picture of me—slipping and stumbling through the snow, protected from the sharp zero wind by mens' long underwear, wool socks, flannel shirt, jeans, wool sweater, heavy wool jacket, four-buckle overshoes, home-made fur-lined mittens, wool cap with a bill and white cottontail tail on top, and a child's old blue wool petticoat pinned around my face! (No wonder I fell down so much!)

Of course the cold tractor would never start with the starter and we didn't dare take a chance on getting kicked again, so we proceeded to "warm her up." This was accomplished by igniting gasoline which had been poured over ashes in a snow shovel and holding it (my job) under the motor pan, while Clark descended the steep hill to the creek for a bucket of icy water. Upon returning, he had to set the water on a sagebrush bonfire to warm before pouring it into the radiator.

Then if all went well and the motor started on the second or third try, I opened the gate into the hay field to let Clark drive through and manipulate the trailer backward into the stack yard, to a handy position beside the haystack. At the sound of the tractor, the cattle started climbing the hill to the feeding ground from the thickets along the creek where they had sought nightly protection from the wind and snow.

By holding the pitchfork with his left hand and right arm, Clark could throw the hay down from the stack, while I tramped it solidly in the trailer. When the load was completed, Clark stood on top of it with the pitchfork, while I drove the tractor out through the field. My problem was: to stop the tractor on the hill, set the brake, jump down, open the wire gate, shoo the cattle away, climb back onto the slick, iron machine, release the brake, start up real easy so that it wouldn't rear up on its hind wheels (yet fast enough not to kill the motor or spin the wheels and get stuck), and do it quickly before the cattle could get back in the way!

Then Clark started throwing off hay while I drove the tractor and tried: not to get stuck, to stay on the old tracks under the new snow, to dodge sagebrush and boulders, to turn at the right moment to keep from going over the edge of the hill, to not hit the heifers' heels (a sudden stop to keep from breaking their legs also meant upsetting Clark), to speed up for another hill, to not slide sidewise down the other steep wagon trail.

What a relief to alight from that machine and start plodding homeward—but not until the water was drained from the radiator, and the cows and calves all counted to be sure that none were gone or sick in the snow. We arrived back to the house each day around noon, tired and cold with housework still waiting.

Where is the woman who said, "My isn't it great to just sit and sew all day long, with the children all in school!"

Or where is the male dinner guest who looked out of the window at the big snow flakes floating downward and exclaimed, "Boy, what a life! Just sitting here by the fire all day and watching it snow."

March 10 Home Made Bread

When I try serving bakery bread and rolls for a change now and then, my family all complain, saying, "Don't put that old stuff in my lunch," and "I don't want any toast made out of the boughten bread," and "Isn't there any of your bread left?"

So, the day when those six big loaves emerge from the oven rolls around quite regularly. While the weather is cool, I use the old, wood-burning range so that I can bake all of the loaves in the big oven at once, and simmer dried corn or ham and beans on top of the stove at the same time.

My recipe is about six times as large as the ordinary cook book recipe. This leaves extra dough to roll up with butter, sugar, and cinnamon and bake in a pan of cream and brown sugar for those "gooey" kind of cinnamon rolls.

April 2 Homestead

"Today we'll have to go get that red cow that won't claim her calf," Clark announces at the breakfast table.

So, later we hitch the stock trailer to the pickup, lead the saddle horse into the trailer (lucky we have a horse that isn't afraid of the trailer), and take off for the Eighty. When we arrive there, Clark mounts the horse and rides up the trail in search of the cattle, while I wander over to the thicket around the big spring to spend my time waiting for him.

The wild thorns are blooming white, the willows and currants are leafing, tiny, green growth of all kinds is covering the black soil. A wild cherry tree is putting forth delicate white clusters of blossoms near the wooden water trough while, underneath, the yellow violets and blue woolly breeches are speckling the green grass.

Reflectively, I climb the hill to look at the stone foundation on the knoll where my mother's homestead cabin stood years ago. How much longer will the gnarled old locust trees, which she planted, live? I rest on a rough, weather-stained rock in the spring sunshine, and look down over the little, fertile valley. Beyond the winding, rushing creek, tractors are busy in the farm fields. The sweetness of the yellow buck-brush and dobey weed blossoms is in the air. A meadowlark whistles from the top of a sagebrush, out-tuning a magpie that is chattering over a bulky, new nest made of sticks in a lone thorn tree. A big hawk sails and circles down from Bald Mountain. Across the valley and beyond in all directions, blue and green mountains rise, some with snowy tips.

An hour passes before the peace of the countryside is broken by the bawling of frisky, white-face calves and cows scampering down around the mountain through the blue sagebrush. Clark has the weak calf on the saddle in front of him. We drive the cattle over to the wire gate and pickup, where Clark finally lands a lariat loop over the red cow's head. Then after pushing and pulling and switching, we do get her up into the trailer with the door locked, load the calf and saddle horse into the pickup and head for home.

April 20 Rocks

Never knew so much dirt could be removed from a hole eight by ten by seven feet. Clark shoveled and shoveled and shoveled and shoveled to make a hole under the edge of the cabin large enough to hold an electric water pump with storage tank and a hot water heater.

When we finally decided that it was deep enough, we started hauling rocks in the pickup to rick up on the inside of the hole for sturdy walls. Rocks, rocks, rocks! I thought we never would find enough flattish rocks. Today, after so many trips, we got the pickup stuck in mud at the end of the house. Then (to make us feel just grand!) here came two men to get the cement mixer which we had borrowed, struggled to unload, and had all set up ready to turn. The owner had suddenly and unexpectedly decided that he wanted to use it.

But we struggled on, and, before the day closed, had the truck dislodged from the mud hole, and another mixer located and borrowed from a neighbor who lives nine miles away.

April 21 Rattly Bang

All day long I have either: thrown big shovelfuls of cement and big shovelfuls of river sand and big bucketfuls of water into the mixer and watched it churn (thank goodness, it runs with an electric motor); or poured the heavy, sloppy mixture into buckets and handed it down into the hole to Clark, who poured it onto the rocks he was stacking to make them stick together in a more substantial wall; or selected the right shape and size of rocks needed and rolled them clattering and screeching down the tin chute into the hole.

After sizing up the job tonight, it seems as though we have only made a beginning.

May 4 Pump for Sale

In spite of the rain and slick, boggy mud, we finally finished the rock walls; and the cautious job of lowering the electric pump and tank and big hot water heater into the hole; and the measuring, cutting, and fitting of pipes.

Says I, "I thought we could save ourselves a lot of work by installing a pressure system, but, considering all the toil of installation, now I'm not so sure!"

At last the miraculous has happened—the water runs from pipes—we no longer have to pump it by hand at the sink and carry it over to fill the tea kettle or the reservoir on the back of the stove in order to have hot water for washing.

May 12 Automatic Versus

Ah, what could be sweeter to the ears of a ranch wife than the whir of an automatic washer!

Think what wash day was like for me until we installed the pressure system and this washer. Oh, not quite rub-a-dub in a tub; however, the water had to be pumped by hand into buckets, poured into a wash boiler, heated on the wood-burning range, redipped into buckets and carried out doors and poured into the washing machine and tubs. If the weather was cold, the machine and equipment were carried into the kitchen.

Now I toss a load of soiled clothes and some washing powder into the machine, turn the button, and let the washing proceed alone while I attend to other work. Why shouldn't I call her my hired girl? For me, no pumping, no lifting of water or heavy wet clothes, no muddy or slick floors, no steamy windows, no moving of bunglesome equipment, no dirty water to empty, no tubs and benches to clean, no long, tiresome wash days.

What would my Grandmother Bean, who reared seven boys and spun all of the thread for their clothes, or my Grandmother Ramey, who started her family of ten children in a sod shanty on the frontier, have thought of such a washing machine as this?

May 15 "Tap Tap Tap"

A flicker hammering under the eaves woke us before the 5:30 alarm this morning. I had to get up and rap on the window to scare it away, and have been repeating this alarm system now and then all day. These long-billed birds, once they get started, are so persistent in pecking round, two-inch holes in buildings that some ranchers shoot them on sight.

But it doesn't seem like spring to me until I hear their "cuk-cuk-cuk" call, and get a glimpse of their black ties and red mustaches and orange-yellow flash of wings over the thickets. There is a heap of sawdust (or should I say beakdust?) on the ground under an old rotten willow tree down by the creek where they are drilling a cavity for a nest.

June 1 *Non-Autophagous*

Early in the spring while I was riding back in the hills looking for the two work horses, high on a rocky point, I found a tiny white-face calf curled up by a bush. I thought its mother must have gone to the creek for a drink; however, the calf looked so tiny and weak when I stood it up that I was afraid it had been deserted.

Toward evening, Clark, riding up to see if it was still there, found it in the same spot with no cow yet in sight, so he put it across the saddle and carried it down to the flat where a group of heifers were grazing. Seeing the one that had borne the calf, he put it down beside her; but she acted wild and would have nothing to do with the little one. Again he loaded the calf and brought it to the barn; then all of us went down and drove the heifers up to the corral, where Clark managed to rope the mother and let the calf suck, although there was a very little milk.

We kept the mother heifer in the corral, but every night and morning she had to be roped and tied up before the calf could be fed. She kicked and bunted it, and was so furious with everyone that no person dared enter the corral with her until she was tied up, for she would immediately charge with her head down! From the safety of the top corral poles, Clark had to rope her and then pull her up to the hitching post. After a couple of weeks, she quieted down enough for Dan to take over the roping job. In about a month, she was docile enough to stand still when Dan merely stood by her head with a threatening rope.

During all of this time she didn't give enough milk for the calf, so Dan would lead it out to the barn and let it suck one of the milk cow's teats. Its tummy filled up so fast that Dan named it Surge (after that brand of milking machine). Soon the little fellow knew where it was going and would follow at a trot right at Dan's heels. At the end of ten weeks, the heifer suddenly surprised us by deciding that she wanted the calf; she was as careful of it as if it was newly born—chased away the hogs and dogs and started producing enough milk so that the calf could be turned out to pasture with her.

June 15 Australian Blue

The cutest thing around here now is a little Australian shepherd puppy given to us by friends. His coat of gray and black markings are called "blue," but he really looks as though he had been camouflaged. His best sport is lying on the steps barking at and teasing the old collie, and when he runs out to play he looks like a furry toy ball bounding about.

The first thing Dan (the always and forever admirer of any and all dogs) asked when he returned from his trip was, "Did you get the puppy yet?"

July 15 Long Prong

I suppose that most beef-cattle raisers feel it is beneath their dignity to milk cows; however, most of the small-acreage ranchers here on the creek and in the valleys do milk some, at least enough to pay the grocery bill and supply milk, cream, and butter for the table. Most of the little dairy herds are a mixed group similar to ours: Nig—a holstein black with big teats that are hard to milk; Jersey—an old, timid, easy-milking, little, brown jersey; Snowflake—a white cow with one horn knocked off; Guernsey—a white—spotted, mild-mannered, high-butterfat-testing guernsey; Spot—a black and white holstein; Frosty—a half-black holstein with a sprinkling of white; Long Prong—a wall-eyed, long-horned, half-jersey white-face that never fails to take a kick at me!

Each morning and evening they must be milked, and the buckets of warm milk carried to the separator room and poured into the separator bowl. One of us turns the separator crank by hand until the cream has been extracted into a kettle, and big buckets full of white, foamy milk stand ready to be fed to the calves or soured for the pigs. Sound monotonous? Perhaps it is.

I seldom have to help with the milking, only in emergencies, but it is my task to rinse, wash, and scald the cloth strainer and twenty odd-shaped pieces of the separator each morning, and to empty the cream into the big can and wash the buckets. The boys assemble the parts and carry them to the barn each evening, then take them apart and carry them back to the house in the morning.

Since there isn't much time for the task of churning, we order butter from the creamery, delivered by the man who comes for our cream once or twice a week. Sometimes the cows make little profit over the grain and hay they eat; but we do have all of the big glasses of rich, cold milk that we can drink (no coffee at our house), yellow cream for cereals or anything we like, and lots of fresh cottage cheese from the skim milk.

September 1 Soliloquy

"What are you sitting out here on the step for?" Danny wants to know as he passes on his way into the house.

"Oh, I like it out here," I reply.

Then I start wondering, just exactly why do I like to sit out here on this old step in the evening?

The hills to the west, towering above us, are yellow in the moonlight—the house and canyon still wrapped in dark shadows.

The North Star and Dippers are showing brightly through the yet-green, lacy leaves of the black locust tree.

Old Laddie is companionably stretched at my feet, while friendly Gray Tom is purring and rubbing gently against my back.

The soft night wind carries the faint scent of pine smoke down from the north woods.

I hear the milk cows munching on grass in the pasture down beyond the pear trees; and also the frequent, contented grunts of the pigs out for a last, cool, clover snack before bedding down for the night.

All of the singing summer birds have departed, but not the adult garden crickets that keep their rhythmic autumn chorus ringing, as though to outdo the boys' low radio music from the attic.

The sound of rippling creek water comes and goes on the shifting air currents.

September 8 Catsup or Ketchup?

On ketchup day, I have every kettle and dishpan filled with tomatoes and peppers and onions sitting all over the top of and in the oven of my old wood-burning range. Electric cook stoves weren't invented for this!

Soon, I also have juice and pulp and seeds and skins sticking to this and to that, dripping here and dripping there. When a person makes thirty quarts of catsup, there's no use of going into the job in a small way! If you are going to have to make a kitchen mess, you may as well cook one big batch and get it over with.

It takes hours and hours of boiling and stirring to get the juice and puree condensed down to the consistency boys like for pouring over hamburgers and fried potatoes. After all of this, it is almost impossible at the end of the day to taste-test and tell whether enough salt, sugar, vinegar, or spices have been added. The vapor rising into the air off of the bags of whole spices floating in the pans is pleasing to the outdoor members of the family.

Does that sound like a lot of ketchup? The boys complained when I ran out of catsup last winter, so I vowed not to let it happen again.

October 18 — Out of Business

Jimmy decided that Johnny's Berkshire hog business looked quite successful and that he would also like to try raising some pigs. He bought a pretty, little gilt from Johnny (to be paid for later out of profits) and took over the job of weighing her grain and feeding her privately from the other hogs. He took good care of her at farrowing time, but was rather disappointed when she had only five pigs. However, everything went well with them until today, when he came home and found his gilt lying dead by the side of the road where a big truck had struck her.

"Well, that settles it," he mourned. "I'm quitting the pig business for good."

October 30 — Farm to Market

Thirty years ago the county road then running by and through our place was nearly impassable throughout the muddy part of the winter months. Mail was carried by sled, buggy, or horseback. In the summertime the road was hard, but rough and narrow with sharp, hairpin turns. Improvement of the road started as a W.P.A. project, then every year a little more straightening and widening and graveling was done, until this fall we saw the hard asphalt surface placed right to our driveway.

This is quite an economic improvement to our part of the county, making the year around trucking of livestock and feeds possible, repair and delivery service obtainable, emergency trips to doctor and hospital quicker, and business and pleasure trips less racking to cars and their occupants. The upper valley children will no longer have to be sent away to town to attend high school, since a school bus can now make the sixty-six-mile round trip to the nearest high school, which is important to us because Johnny can be home at nights.

November 21 — Prickly Plumage

When Berky sow found a dead porcupine on the road where a car had run over it, she tried to eat it, with the result that her nose, mouth, tongue, and throat were stuck full of quills.

It was a dreadful job for all of us to help hold her, pry her mouth open and, with long-handled pliers, pull out the tenacious quills. We wondered if she would die, for we couldn't reach all that were in her throat, and knew that she must have swallowed several. However, the county agent assured us that the quills weren't likely to harm her unless they worked into her heart.

A few days later she had a big litter of pigs, and, so far, seems to be feeling fine.

November 30 Sad Seeds

We mowed our first alfalfa hay on the Eighty this summer, then, hoping to make a neat sum from the seed crop, we let it grow and develop blossoms.

But a long drought cut the growth short and, worst of all, the grasshoppers increased by the millions. We bought some poison dust and, with a dusting machine, dusted the best of the plants in the central area; but more hoppers kept moving down from the arid hills onto the green growth. The fragile, purple blossoms appeared to be the hoppers' favorite delicacy.

A few, belated blossoms did manage to mature late in the season, and we went down with the tractor and old mower to cut what seed we could find. Clark pitched the dry stalks into small bunches behind while I drove the tractor. Except for running over a big rock (which Clark had explicitly warned me to avoid) and breaking the wooden tongue out of the mower (it took half a day to make and install a new one), I did all right.

Ominous dark clouds kept appearing over the southern horizon, causing me to wonder if showers would come before we could get the seeds dried and threshed. Sure enough, the long-needed rain did come, day after day, mildewing and beating our precious seeds onto the ground.

When at last the rain was over, and the bunches dry enough to haul to the threshing machine, little came out but faded chaff— only three short sacks of seed, not enough to pay for our harvesting expenses.

December 10 Golden Grains

On grain-grinding day I always think: "I sure don't want to grind that old grain today." But after we get started, even though the air is somewhat dusty and chilly, I rather enjoy dipping up bucketfuls of the yellow grains of wheat and barley and watching them sink down the hopper into the grinder to fall out with a refreshing redolence that no other product can boast of except newly ground grain.

The grinder and tractor motor (by which the grinder is powered) make such a loud, clangorous noise that Clark and I have to shout at each other when necessary. The rest of the time is spent carrying grain and thinking our own thoughts until the little granary bin is full of chopped grain feed.

It was on one of these days while watching the wheat roll, that the inspiration suddenly came to me to start writing a book. Now I ask you, would beans or buttermilk have caused the same daydream? Or *nightmare*?

— YEAR OF 1952 —
SUMMER OF SNAKES

January 12 Mail S(n)ack

I often wonder if city families get as much daily pleasure from incoming mail as we do.

Around noon every weekday, we begin to keep an eye and an ear turned toward the hillside west of the house where the highway runs. We want to see the Star Route mail carrier when he drives by and throws our mail sack into the box; waste no time in going after it—who knows what treasures a mail sack may hold?

Always there is the daily paper out of Boise with its "funnies"; and as we subscribe to fifteen periodicals, more or less, there is a good chance of receiving a magazine—perhaps Clark's weekly *Saturday Evening Post,* or Dan's *Outdoor Life,* or Johnny's *Berkshire News,* or Jimmie's *Mechanix Illustrated,* or my *Reader's Digest,* or a cheerful farm magazine.

We receive leaflets from the College of Agriculture on farm electrification, illustrated pamphlets from feed and implement companies. We hear about local activities, arrests, scandals, births, weddings, deaths, socials, sales from our weekly county newspaper. Of course, the most delightful items are personal letters from friends and relatives.

Twice a year we receive a big, thick catalogue from Sears Roebuck and one from Montgomery Ward, and, more often, sale and seed catalogues. Even the numerous circulars aren't all dull if one wants to waste time reading them.

A package might arrive (even though it isn't Christmas), as sometimes we do shop from the catalogues or order from Boise. Then, too, I belong to a home research staff which sends sampling products.

In the mail today came a package of instant coffee. Now I wonder how a family which never drinks coffee can test and compare the flavors? When I try serving or giving this often-sent, said instant coffee to friends or relatives, they almost appear to be insulted! Say, why couldn't that little, square, cardboard box in the mail sack be fancy cheeses or sardines, Clark would like to know?

January 17 Call for Home Economist

In the mail today, I received a circular asking me to subscribe to a farm magazine which would delight me with up-to-the-minute articles on re-decorating, hobbies, travel and vacations, patterns and clothing styles, beauty hints, recipes and menus, needlework and crochet, and child care.

I laughed at how these appealing ideas did not apply to me—not that it is really a laughing matter.

Take, for instance, the item of re-decorating: I have no problems with rugs, drapes, wallpapers, or furniture arrangements; in fact, we have no dining room, living room, bedrooms, or bath—just one all-purpose room. Even if the word were "remodeling," we haven't a house worth re-building.

Consider travel and vacations: completely out of our life—we are lucky if we find time now and then to go to the timber for a picnic.

Needlework and crochet: any time that I can find for the needle goes into shirt and overall patching, or maybe a new pair of pajamas.

Patterns and clothing styles: what, in all likelihood, happens when I decide to wear a house dress for the day? I am unexpectedly called to chase cows or pigs through weeds and stickers and thorns which scratch my legs (nylon hose are unmentionable); my skirt accidently swirls into the manure or bucket of water when I go to feed the hens; somewhere I manage to come in contact with a barbed wire (which loves to tear three-cornered holes in dresses), insects or nettles or icy winds (also fond of bare legs), drops of muddy irrigation water (how it does amuse them to spatter-paint on gingham); suddenly I am called to the shop to help hold a black, greasy piece of machinery. In order to protect my disposition, as well as dresses, I cling to blue jeans, blouses, sturdy oxfords, and anklets, perhaps ninety-five percent of the daylight hours. I feel that a person in my circumstances can't afford to invest much time or money in the other five percent of the time spent in wearing dresses. (Perhaps the biggest crisis in the matter of clothing came when I received an invitation to my niece's June church wedding in Boise. It almost made me ill trying to decide whether or not to attend. The only hat and gloves in the house that would match my tan sport dress, slippers, and skin were Dan's brown cowboy hat and leather gauntlets! I rejected that idea, not wanting to take all of the attention from the beautiful bride. Finally, I did decide to go—and, incidently, found guests attired in various styles—but, afterward, I wondered if I did the right thing in publicly greeting my aunts. They looked so very proper and fragile in white accessories, and I—well, you've heard of that brown country flavor!. . . under a borrowed hat!)

Child care: this is for the mothers of tiny tots.

Beauty hints: It would take more than hints to keep my hair presentable after mashing down the curls with a wool cap or hot sun helmet. And if I used only half the time advised on hair, skin, nails, eyebrows, make-up, teeth, and beauty exercises, I wouldn't have time left for the routine chores.

Hobbies: more now than I have time to cultivate. The main one, writing, goes weeks and months at a time without a written word.

Recipes and menus: Everyone has to eat, so this should be a welcome item. I'll admit that sometimes I do look hopefully through the appetizing menus pictured but, in ninety-eight percent of the recipes, there are food items included which I do not have stocked on my shelves, do not have time to drive to town to obtain, or cannot afford. Mostly, my menus are planned around the foods which we produce on the farm, with enough staples and extras from the grocery store to insure nutritional balance. The boys like plain butter or cream-flavored vegetables and fresh, juicy meats brought hot from the kitchen range, and not appetizers nor soup-mixed concoctions nor over-fancy salads and deserts. In fact, none of the time-consuming recipes that I have been unfortunate enough to try have brought the family praise that the magazine suggested they would, and some pictured beauties have been downright sickening. (Just ask the boys about the big, molded, asparagus-tip salad we tried when we lived in California!)

February 17 As Ye Sow

Seed catalogues come early so that "green thumbers" have ample time to dream over the fascinating new varieties while the snow is piled high and there is, supposedly, leisure time before the spring rush.

By trial and error, my selection of seeds has narrowed down to those vegetables which do well here, and the ones we like best to eat.

The hours of summer heat here in the canyon where the sun rises late and sets early are too few to provide good flavor in cantaloupes and early watermelons. Late watermelons are fine if the frost doesn't get them. The season usually isn't long enough to fully mature popcorn, peanuts, celery, and tomatoes. Dried beans such as garbanzo, lima, navy, and red Mexicans don't produce enough mature beans before frost to pay to plant. The eggplants' purple glow adds beauty to the garden, but we found that we liked summer squash, sliced and fried, just as well, and it is much quicker and easier to grow.

Kale and broccoli grow well, but I failed to find a safe way of removing the hoards of aphids from the curly green leaves. Aphids ruined the turnips, also. Perhaps I could have sprayed them, but I dislike using anything more poisonous than rotenone dust. Curly top disease prevents good growth of tampala, spinach, beets and swiss chard.

I planted ground cherries to show the boys what queer fruits they were, but do you think they would eat the preserves I made from them? Neither did they like okra nor Chinese cabbage nor parsnips. Jimmy raised a row of giant sun-flowers, which were grand to admire, but not much of an asset in the way of food.

I doubt, though, if a gardener ever lived who didn't try at least one new variety each year, if he could get it. Right now I wonder—those pictures look especially tempting of kohlrabi, parsley, brussels sprouts, sweet potatoes, mustard, garlic, rutabagas—and I haven't tried them yet!

I received four different catalogues—from Boise, from Iowa, from California, and from Oregon. This gives a wide variety of seeds and climates from which to select. For instance, I take up my colorful Iowa catalogue and read the glowing descriptions of the dark red, sweet beets; then I consult my bulletin from the University of Idaho on vegetable varieties for Idaho gardens for correct varieties to use in this locality. None of the Iowa beets are listed! I do find two of the California ones listed, but, upon referring back to the bulletin, find that they are not the proper kind for canning. I look in the Boise book, but they haven't the right ones either. I examine the Oregon catalogue and do find three of the listed ones and at a lower price; but also see advertised a new variety developed especially to resist curly top disease. Boy, that is just exactly what I need, so I get out the order blank.

Thus I go 'round and 'round with some twenty different vegetables—and then often find the ones I need at the local seed store.

Yes, it takes time to pour over the merits of the latest hybrids and make the weighty decisions as to the best. It is a mighty good thing that the seed companies have the foresight to send the enticing catalogues early.

March 30 The (C)old Swimming Hole

Clark started counting the cattle on the hillsides across the creek while he was throwing hay out of the barn at the Lower Place, and I was tramping it down in the wagon.

"Isn't that a cow by that bush up next to the rim? If it is, why doesn't it move?" he wondered.

Then I started watching it, and decided that it was a cow with a white-face calf bobbing around her in the rocks. All of the other cattle had started back down toward the feed grounds while we were feeding, so Clark decided to ride up to see if the cow was all right.

I said I'd sit by the barn and wait, in case he needed me. All of the time I was thinking, "Why do those silly cows have to cross the creek to have their calves? I wish we had a fenced-in feed lot so that calves wouldn't have to be carried back on the saddle." I wandered out onto a steep point, high above the creek, and sat on a big rock.

Clark lifted his feet out of the stirrups to keep from getting them wet, but suddenly the water came up around his waist and the horse was swimming! Clark jumped off on the upstream side and held onto the saddle horn but lost the reins. Just as they were nearing the opposite shore (and I could almost catch my breath again) the foolish old horse turned and headed right back through the deepest and rockiest part of the creek, with Clark on the down-stream side. That didn't look good, so Clark let go and scrambled ashore.

When the horse neared my side of the stream, I suddenly came to life and ran down the rough trail to catch him. Just beyond my reach, about six feet out in the current, he stopped to paw furiously at the water and would come no closer to me. Luckily, I found a willow stick with a broken crotch at one end that was long enough for me to use to reach out and snag the bridle reins.

The horse under control again, I glanced across the creek to see Clark wringing the icy water from his clothes. He motioned for me to take the horse up the creek to a better crossing. When I reached the place, I unbuttoned my coat and removed my overshoes and climbed into the saddle, thinking, "How can he expect me to cross this high water? But maybe he thinks this will be safe up here where there aren't so many holes and rocks."

We were only a few feet out into the water when I heard Clark yelling above the roar of the angry water, "Hey! hey! Don't you try to ride across. Go back!" Sometimes some words can be *so* welcome! We quickly retraced Prince's wading steps and I re-donned my overshoes. "Send him across by himself," Clark ordered. Where he ever got such an idea, I cannot imagine. I think Prince feared the cold, raging water nearly as much as I; up and down the bank he would go, but not across.

"Take him down below the barn and try him there," came the next instructions. Although it wasn't hard for me to ride down there in a few minutes, Clark had to climb a steep mountain trail above sheer cliffs and back down again to reach this crossing which I knew to be deep. Of course, Prince was just as stubborn as ever, and Clark came up with the next decision, "If I take off my boots, I think I can swim it!"

I protested, I begged, I argued, I pleaded, "Please, please, don't try to swim it! You might get cramps in this cold water. If it swept you around the bend, it would dash you to pieces against the rocks. Walk down to the bridge, and I'll come after you in the car. Or walk up the creek, it's only six miles to that bridge. Or go up the mountain east, it wouldn't take me long to come and get you." (It would have been only 25 or 30 miles round trip!)

But no, he rejected it all! "You don't know what an awful trip that would be down that canyon," he called back across the noisy water. He waded out onto a big rock, slipped into the water up to his waist again, then waded back out.

"Well," I retorted in despair, "I guess you'll do whatever you want to. I can't stand to watch you, and I can't help you. I'm going home." I started up the hill leading the horse. I looked back once to see him wringing water from his clothes again. Just as I reached the county road, I heard a faint, "YO HO!" and, looking back down the mountain and across the creek, saw him walking north and motioning that way.

I thought I would sit by the fire a few minutes after reaching the house, then drive up the road to the nearest bridge and wait for him. Soon I heard a step on the porch, and he walked through the door, dripping wet again!

He said, "I tried the crossing up here north of the barn—didn't even have to swim, just waded all the way across!"

Was it a calf, or was it not? Who cares.

April 12 Chinee

While we were feeding hay at the Lower Place yesterday, we thought we could see a cow lying in a boggy spot below a spring on the hill west. Clark rode up and found it to be a young holstein cow that I had named Chinee because black and white markings, resembling Chinese writing, streaked her face. She was lying in the mud, too weak to get up. Clark pulled her around onto more solid ground, with her head uphill, until she managed to pull herself onto her feet. As it was too far to drive her back to the barn in her weakened condition, he left her to graze on the few wisps of green grass coming through.

I sat on the leeward side of the old rickety barn, where I could watch him while he rode back to get her this morning. He rode up around an immense fresh dirt slide, and started the cow back the same way. But she was bound to take a short cut back across the dirt slide and he couldn't stop her. I held my breath! I suppose rock and earth slides that have stabilized are safe, but these looked as though they might start sliding again at any moment.

Chinee was about two thirds of the way across when her foot slipped in the softened soil, and down she rolled, over and over and over, finally stopping about forty-five feet from the creek which was the foot of the slide. Clark was leaping down after her, and I started on the run to help him. When I got there, he was holding onto her tail to keep her from rolling again, but he couldn't get her up. The trouble was that we had raised her at the barn—what we call a bucket calf—and she was too gentle to be afraid of our threats and too weak to want to get up.

We considered tying a rope to the saddle horse and trying to drag her out, but decided against it, as the mountain was so steep and the footage so soft in the slide, that we might also lose the horse. After more deliberation, we let her slip on down into the creek, hoping that when her feet hit solid rock she would stand up and wade along the edge of the water until she could find a way out. Instead of that, the water swept her down the creek! She bobbed slowly up and down, swimming just enough to bring her ashore on the other side several rods downstream. She landed on her feet, but there were bushes all around her, and instead of trying to find a way out, she just stood there looking back at us, as though to say, "Well, aren't you coming to get me out?"

The water was too high to take a chance on riding the horse across, so when we arrived back at the house, Clark, hoping to drag her out with the horse and lariat, crossed above the barn and rode the two miles back down on the other side of the creek. But when he got there, she was gone, evidently washed away down the canyon.

April 20 Women Traders

Today has found me setting out a big box of strawberry plants given to me by a neighbor friend on a Sunday visit. That is one of the joys of owning a place in the country—exchanging plants with neighbors. Flower trading, the most favored indulgence, is somewhat out of my line because, with no irrigation system for our yard, only the sturdiest of plants can survive the dry summer months and come back to bloom the following spring. With no lawn, we allow the weeds, wild grass, alfalfa, and hardy flowers to grow in profusion rather than to have bare ground and dust.

But I have been grateful to receive the start of blackberries, bush cherries, multiplier onions, strawberries, black raspberries, the lovely bearded irises with the romantic names, ash and black walnut trees, and forsythias. In return I have had pleasure in giving old and new irises; butter-and-eggs; orange poppies; onion sets; black raspberries; tomato, cabbage, and broccoli plants; hollyhock seeds.

In the same amicable way, we exchange fruits and vegetables when we have the opportunity. If a woman has a surplus of berries, cherries, or peaches, she sends word to another, who perhaps has none. Later, in return, she may receive pickling cucumbers, string beans, tomatoes, or dill. One day in harvest time, friends drove in with the back of their car heaped full of apples; they returned home with squashes and lard from our cellar.

May 4 Ah, When Roundup Day Is Over

Early this morning we were again herding cows and calves together and starting them on their southward journey. The sad part of it was that, as we didn't have time to mark the calves yesterday, we had to stop them at a range corral along the way and do the job today. It really is a sad job for me. I wish someone would invent painless ways of working with cattle.

Here is the whole revolting process: While the branding irons are heating in a sage brush bonfire, we herd all of the cows and calves into a corral, then gradually eliminate the cows by opening a gate and running them out, one by one. In this merry-go-round melee, a calf sometimes dashes out and has to be retrieved. When at last the calves are all separated from the cows, we go to the pickup to get the veterinary supplies we have brought along, and I build up the fire while Clark fills the vaccinating needles. Again we climb up over the corral poles to the inside of the corral where Clark ropes a calf and throws it to the ground. Then I put a loop of the rope around its back feet and tie the other end tautly to a post, while Clark ropes the front feet and ties that rope to a post in the opposite direction. The result—calf is stretched out on its left side so that it cannot get up.

I fetch the vaccinating needles to Clark, for the calves must have shots to guard against blackleg, malignant edema, and hemorrhagic septicemia. Next comes the caustic pencil (with cotton to protect fingers) to rub around the base of the horn button to stop its growth and make it fall off. If the horns have grown too large, they may have to be cut off with the dehorners, or, if too large for that, a dehorning saw. If blood squirts from the head, the offending blood vessels have to be grasped and pulled out with the artery pliers. We sprinkle blood-stopper powder on the horn wounds, which also helps to keep away blow flies whose eggs cause maggots within the head.

Then I carry over the bucket of lysol water containing the emasculators to be used on all of the male calves. With a sharp pocket knife, Clark cuts off the end of the right ear and a notch on the under-side of the left ear. Now it is time for me to climb out over the corral bars and hand the hot branding iron in to be pressed onto the calf's hide directly over the right ribs. The calf bawls horribly, rolls its eyes, and struggles while the smoke and stench of burning hide and hair rises into the dusty air. At last the bloody little creature is untied and, when it jumps up, we open the gate to let it run through to its mother. What a sigh of relief from me when the corral is empty and we gather up our tools.

About the time we get the cattle started down the highway again, a neighbor stops his car to tell us that another herd of cattle is coming from that direction a few miles down. Soon three or four people have brought the troublesome news, but there is little we can do about it because calves can walk only so fast and there are few dodging spaces along the road. We have to continually watch for calves that wander to the side of the road and lie down behind sage brush. Sometimes, if a calf can't keep up with the rest of the herd, we load it into the pickup; but then the mother cow is hard to drive, because she thinks she has lost her calf and wants to run back to look for it. One of us rides Prince while the other walks back and forth helping to drive the cattle and the pickup by relays.

Toward evening we reach our pasture lane about five minutes ahead of the other herd. Thank goodness! We made it without the calamitous mixup that would have resulted, had they met.

I run ahead to open the wire gate and count the calves as they go through. One calf short! Clark thinks surely that I have made a mistake in counting, but I am just as sure that I have not. We drive back, looking closely on all sides. We get the boys who are now home from school and drive back again. Suddenly someone spots a bit of white below a boulder. We stop and cautiously slip up and grab the calf before it gets alerted. (We learned this lesson on our first drive—when we walked over to get that calf, it took off down over hills like a jackrabbit. After nearly a mile of continual running up hill and down dale, Johnny managed to grab it on a creek meadow straightaway, and to hold it down until we could drive closer with the car and bring a rope.)

We take the calf back to the pasture, put it with the cattle which are munching the new grass they have been so hungry for, and watch until we are quite sure it has found its mother. Then we drop a block of salt into the salt trough, load the horse into the pickup, and head for home to tend the milk cows, bucket calves, little chickens, and to prepare supper. What a day!

May 8 Land Clearing

It doesn't take much brush grubbing and rock removing to make a person realize how our pioneers toiled to prepare the land for cultivation.

By the creek on the Lower Place, we have a little meadow pasture that has been growing smaller, caused by the encroachment of willow shoots and driftwood along one side. Today, Clark and I assumed the task of re-clearing it. He chopped and grubbed willows while I carried off armloads of loose pieces and threw them in piles along the edge of the creek. We never burn any brush which can be used to stabilize the banks and prevent the washing away of precious loam. We sprinkled chlordane dust over the big, red ant mounds that we tore down. When at last we stood back to survey our work, we were well pleased with its smooth appearance, and knew that there would be less grievance when the mowing machine made its rounds in July.

We sat on the stone-boat to eat our lunch. The stone-boat is a wooden sledge made specifically for hauling rocks from fields. Being without wheels and low to the ground, rocks can quite easily be rolled onto it—that is, if any kind of rock handling can be called easy. We spent the afternoon driving the team and pulling the stone-boat around and around the fields, stopping here and there to load on rocks that have mysteriously cropped up in the soil. We rolled them off at spots along the creek where high water has been assiduously lapping away our black soil.

At evening our gloves were worn out and part of the skin from our fingers. Never-the-less, it was a good day.

May 11 Farrowing Day

I dump the breakfast dish water, put on an old heavy jacket, hurry to the barn, look over the board panel into the pig pen.

Oh, oh, Berky already has three newborn pigs. Quickly I gather up a burlap sack, scissors, and iodine from a shelf; connect the electric cord to the heat lamp; climb over the board panel into the pen; pet the sow to stop her from getting excited. The wiggly, little pig which I pick up is as hard to hold as a slick, live fish but, after several attempts, I do get it slightly cleaned with the sack and clip the naval cord and "dab on" some iodine. Then I place it in a clean nest of straw under the warm heat bulb in a boarded-in corner of the pen. This procedure keeps the little ones from dying of chill before they are dry, or from getting mashed under the heavy sow. I take care of the other two, then seat myself on a one-legged milk stool beside a couple of bales of straw to await the arrival of more pigs.

Hours pass. The south wind is blowing around the eaves and through the cracks between the boards, making the lariat and strings sway on the hanging saddle. Up on the rafters, the English sparrows are chirping. I gaze out over the manger at the morning sunshine glistening on the rolling water of the creek close below. Beyond the creek, with its edging of new, yellow-tinged willow leaves, cows and horses are grazing on the hillsides; while far to the north, the timbered mountains rise majestically white to accent the dark green leaves of the near thorn trees. Occasionally, a mourning dove's soft cooing on the roof sounds, in total contrast to the groaning and teeth snapping of the sow.

Now and then I rescue another pig, or walk over to peek into the brooder at the tiny, black, pug-nosed, white-footed, wriggling Berkshires rooting each other around in the straw.

After the sow has her tenth and last pig, I open the brooder and let the little hungry fellows out to nurse. How they scramble and bite and squeal at each other as they fight greedily for the nipples of warm milk! When they begin to drowse off with contented stomachs, I push them back into the brooder (which is about as hard as getting ants into a nest) and fasten the door. Within a few hours they will have learned to run into the warm corner by themselves, to sleep side by side as close as sardines packed in a can.

Am I glad to have that task completed—now I can return to the house and a bath. Johnny will soon be home from school to look after his own project. I will gladly leave to him the chore of clipping the pigs' sharp needle teeth and notching their ears for identification and registration.

May 15 Reconnoitering

"It is Sunday. What shall we do today?" the boys wanted to know after breakfast and morning chores were over.

"We haven't been down to see about the heifers for over a week. Shall we do that?" I ask them. They all agreed that that would be fun, so we loaded up the saddle horse, climbed into the pickup and took off for the Eighty.

We all enjoy looking at the cattle. This is the time of the year when they shed the old, long, faded, woolly, matted hair and grow a new, sleek, short, summer coat. Fat curves are replacing the lean winter look. Following the cows are frisky little calves with snowy white faces, and the yearlings grow so fast and change appearance so much that they look strange even to us. On horseback Clark can ride right up to the cattle, but if they see us afoot, they run like deer. From a bag tied onto the saddle, we took two forty pound blocks of iodized salt and left them in troughs for the cattle to lick.

As we also wanted to inspect our coming hay crop, we walked on through the knee-deep alfalfa. We watched the wind blowing through the dark green leaves of the fifty acres of Ranger alfalfa and thought, "What a wonderful legume it is to produce so abundantly on dry land."

We strolled on over to the old house where Clark and I spent our first four years of married life. The paper is hanging down from the ceilings, the window broken, screens torn, groundhog holes dug under the rock foundation. In the yard an old, broken cream separator lies forlornly on its side and the old crab apple tree by the back porch has toppled over. One ancient apple tree is blossoming beside the trickling water from the spring. The old-fashioned yellow roses that, years before, I had set by the path have spread, and the locust seedling I planted by the gate now makes a deep shade over rank, wild grass. Part of the big dug-out cellar (that we were so proud of at the time

Clark's father helped to build it with a team of horses) has fallen in. My garden, where once the Mormon crickets devoured everything, is now overtaken with milk weed and plum thicket.

I wandered up to look at the little hen house that Clark had built for my prize leghorns; but, when I stepped on a loose board hidden under tall weeds, I instantly detected the odor of skunk. Retreated in haste! By the cold spring amid a grove of wild plums and lombardy poplars, we saw honey bees busily flying in and out of a hole in an old, dead poplar.

On our way back to the pickup, we gathered big bouquets of wild, yellow and lavender lupine, my favorite, and wished we had brought a picnic lunch so that we could have stayed all day.

July 11 Poison

I wasn't sorry to see old Long Prong dismissed from the dairy barn to take over the task of raising an extra calf along with her own. Her jersey blood must cause her to produce rich milk, as both calves grew fast—big and sturdy.

Yesterday, I noticed her white calf standing in a rather dazed way, not bothering to graze; later it began to bawl and run around in circles before it finally fell in convulsions and died.

The veterinarian to whom we sent a description of the symptoms sent back word for us to look around for a source of poison, probably white lead in paint. We went straight to the granary and looked under it for a stored can of white lead. We found it, all right, but not under the granary. The pigs had rooted it out into the barnyard and dislodged the lid—the contents were dried hard, but evidently the calf had licked enough to cause its death.

One of the drawbacks of the livestock industry is that so much money is lost on the animals that perish before reaching maturity or the market. As an example, out of the nine heifers to which we fed straw the first winter we were here, only four are left. One died when it wandered off the feed yard one night and broke its leg in a badger hole; another died when she tried to give birth to a calf with her back down hill; one was found dead not far from the road during hunting season; the fifth we decided was stolen, as she entirely disappeared from the Eighty, leaving a young calf.

July 20 To Market, to Market

Berky must go. All of us are sad to have to part with such a gentle barnyard pet, but such partings are an inevitable part of ranch life.

Her male pigs, and also those of her gilts, have had so many ruptures that, after gathering all available material on the subject, we have decided it must be an inherited tendency. Therefore, Johnny is selling all of them and replacing with registered gilts bred in the midwest from high producing lines.

July 30 Farmhand

Haying went into high gear this summer when the long rains, which caused the creek to run high and the hay to grow abundantly, finally ceased for a few days. Some new equipment of our own, and more made available by pooling labor and machinery with a neighbor, helped get the eighty tons of hay on The Eighty stacked before the showers came again.

This year instead of throwing the hay onto the wagon with pitch forks, they gathered it into large bunches with a buckrake—a big-tined scoop mounted on the front of the tractor—then pushed it close to the stackyard. Next the bunches were gathered up, one by one, and lifted and dumped onto the stack with another big-tined machine, the Farmhand, which can raise a load high into the air.

A fairly level spot had to be located on which to build the stack to keep the Farmhand from tipping over when lifting the loads. Johnny, who operated the tractor and Farmhand all summer, was careful and lucky enough to keep it sitting right-side up.

More rain nearly ruined the rest of our hay. It delayed the cutting past blossom time—which lowers the protein content—then, after it was cut and before it could be dried and stacked, most of the leaves fell off, leaving blackened stems. On top of that, the grasshoppers hatched out by the millions and now we will have to turn the cattle into the fields in order to garner any benefit from the second growth.

August 10 Snakes Alive

We were preparing for bed last night when an unusual din sounded over the noise of the running bath water. The Australian pup seemed to be barking viciously at something under the elm tree. Wondering if someone had dropped another cat in our driveway, I glanced out of the door just in time to see the pup suddenly jump straight into the air and bound toward the house. Then he made big, barking circles around the danger spot, never again approaching closer than fifteen feet.

"Clark," I suggested, "you still have your shoes on, take this flashlight and see what Blue is barking at."

"Probably nothing but a toad," he muttered, but switched on the light and waded out through the dry grass and weeds. "Can't see a thing," he said.

At about that time I imagined that I heard a queer little cricket noise. "What was that?" I called suspiciously. No answer. "Clark, did you hear anything?"

"Yes," he answered guardedly. "It's a rattlesnake. Get me a shovel."

I dashed out barefooted to the woodshed (fortunately the shovel was there), hurried back, and leaned over as far as possible to hand him the shovel and still keep my feet on the path. "Please be careful," I begged, as I quickly retreated to the porch. "Can you see it?"

"Oh, this darned flashlight! The batteries are all run down. Have we got some new ones?"

"No, I forgot to get them when we were in town," I admitted reluctantly.

"I saw its rattle disappear across this bicycle trail while you were getting the shovel. Now it won't rattle again, and this light is so dim that I can't locate it."

We decided that it would be foolhardy to search around in those weeds in the dark, so he gave up the pursuit. I worried, "How can I ever make myself go down the path through the weeds to the chicken house in the morning, or to the garden, either?"

"Oh, you don't need to worry about that snake," Clark consoled me. "Rattlesnakes won't stay around where people or dogs are. It will be far gone by morning."

Nevertheless, this morning I kept my eyes wide open, walked very slowly and carefully when outside, and caught my breath whenever a dry leaf rustled or a grasshopper jumped. Now, I have lived in these dry, Idaho foothills nearly all of my life, hiking and herding cows and turkeys, but never have I ever run across a rattlesnake. My luck might change, though, because on a cold dewy morning last spring, I had stepped on a bullsnake while hunting asparagus tips.

August 17 Hissing

After three or four days I decided Clark must have been right—evidently the snake had crawled back into the hills. But this morning there was a loud hissing noise just outside the open window.

"Jimmy," I called, "did you forget to turn off the hose when you watered the calves?"

"No, I'm sure I turned if off," he answered.

Cautiously, we walked over to the window and peeked out through the screen. "It sounds like water squirting out of a break in the hose," we agreed.

"All I can see is a white pullet walking under those big sunflowers. Now the noise has stopped. There it goes again."

"Oh, Jimmy, it must be that rattlesnake!"

"And Daddy is gone! What will we do?"

We went outside and slipped carefully around the corner of the house. I had picked up the shovel, but how to use it was the next question. I wouldn't dare get close enough to chop down with it; and that I could throw it straight enough or hard enough was very doubtful. Although the pullet had wandered away, this hissing continued. Finally, amid the dense growth of weeds and flowers, I spied the huge snake about three feet from the house and crawling toward it. My heart was beating fast. I felt weak and wondered if I might faint. "Goodness," I thought, "if I should pass out, he'd get me for sure!"

Just then we heard a car coming on the highway. What a timed miracle! Dan ran to the pickup shouting, "Daddy, come quick. Rattlesnake! Rattlesnake!"

It wasn't long before Clark had some weeds cut away and brought the dead snake out on the shovel. "Well, I'm glad we got him. Now we won't have to worry about it any more," he advised us. "Now that you have all heard a rattlesnake rattle, you will know if you ever hear one again. They all sound alike."

"I've heard that rattlesnakes always travel in pairs," I added, picking up some big clods and tossing them around in the weeds but there was no responsive rattle. "And also that they go blind in August and neglect to rattle at all."

August 23 Another One

I wore rubber boots and carried the shovel to the garden with me for several days until it began to get a little tiresome. Today, however, being in a rush to get an onion for the stew, I forgot all about snakes in my hurry down the hill to the garden.

We had some luscious peaches ripening on a tree by the path, and I was looking up to see how red they were when, "Buzzzzzzzzz," went something directly in front of my feet. Involuntarily, I leaped backward, then looked down at a rattler's tail as he crawled toward a pear tree. I didn't have the shovel, and I didn't dare leave the snake long enough to get one for fear that it would crawl out of sight. Clark was taking a little nap on the cot before supper—if only I could yell loud enough to waken him.

"Clark! Clark! Clark!" I shouted louder and faster, until he came, grabbing the reliable shovel on the way. That old snake must not have been blind, the way he kept rattling and poking his head from behind the burdock leaves to see where I was.

In cutting down the burdock around which the snake was coiled, Clark also cut off the rattling tail. The snake struck only once at the shovel before Clark hit it, but it didn't coil up in a round coil as I had heard they do—it just pulled back into an S shape, then straightened out as it struck. After its head was cut off, Clark held a stick in front of its mouth, and instantly its needle-like fangs unfolded like cat's claws and shot venom onto the stick.

September 8 More Rattlesnake Fallacies

I haven't waded into any more weeds to pick berries or look for pullet eggs.

Another thing Clark informed us, "You won't need to worry if you are riding a horse. Horses are scared to death of rattlesnakes—won't get close to one."

A couple of weeks later Danny came home from riding after cattle down on Cottonwood Creek and said, "I thought I heard an awful big cricket, but when I looked down, there was a rattlesnake striking at Prince's leg!"

"But," I asked, "Didn't the horse jump away?"

"No. The snake missed and I had to whip the horse away quick. He wasn't a bit scared."

"What ever made you think it was a cricket?"

"Why, Mother, it didn't sound a bit like this rattlesnake out here by the house! When I got off to get some rocks to throw on him, he crawled under a big rock, and about that time here came another rattlesnake crawling down the hill. I got that one killed but was scared to touch the boulder that the first one had crawled under for fear he might strike me. So I got my lariat and roped the rock to pull it off of him, but I roped him right in with the rock which cut him in two. Then the rock rolled on top of him and smashed him! I wish I could have brought the rattles home to show you."

"Well, why couldn't you?"

"'Cause the snakes were so cut up and mashed up, and the hill was so steep that the pieces rolled off down in a pile of rocks!"

People have told me, "If you want to get rid of rattlesnakes, turn hogs into the yard." Hummm, who wants hogs in the garden?

Another said, "Drop some china nest eggs around in the weeds. The snakes will swallow them, get indigestion, and die." I wonder.

September 28 Dig That Cellar

The boards and braces in our cellar were beginning to rot, allowing dirt to drop in. Since a fruit and vegetable storage cellar is an essential part of a farmstead, we decided that we would have to remove all of the fruit jars and other stored items, tear out the old timbers, and build a new one. All of this involved plenty of labor, but the hardest part was digging the dirt floor eighteen inches deeper. We wanted to dig the hole larger and pour cement walls so that it couldn't rot down soon again.

Even with a pick it was almost impossible to penetrate the hard clay floor. Finally the boys decided that dynamite was the only solution. I wasn't so sure that it was a wise idea—the house being close, I thought they might blow a hole through it, too. I told them to warn me before each shot, so that I could run up on the hill and hide behind the hay wagon! Fortunately, no harm was done and the clay was broken up in spots. They lifted the loose dirt up into a trailer and pulled it with the tractor to a dumping spot in the pasture.

Suddenly from the pasture I heard Johnny yell, "Daddy! Daddy! Come here quick!" The first thought coming to my mind was the discovery of another rattlesnake. Then Jimmy also took up the frantic call, and I had the sickening thought that they had upset the tractor. We ran as fast as we could go, but our husky hired boy beat us to him, and lifted the loaded trailer from Johnny's leg. How he ever lifted such a weight, I don't know. The leg was broken above the ankle.

Against their daddy's orders, they had detached the trailer from the tractor; when one wheel rolled into a ditch, the trailer knocked Johnny around, and the tongue fell on his leg.

He stayed in the hospital for three days and missed the first two weeks of school. With his entire leg in a stiff cast, what an ordeal the first few days at school were for him—climbing onto the bus, riding twenty-five miles to school, climbing up and down steep stairs to each class on crutches. His morale has been boosted by the kindness of those around him—a bus driver who assigned him a seat just inside the door, teachers who let him into the classrooms early and dismiss him early, a classmate who faithfully carries his books and lunch.

This misfortune slowed down our work, and the cellar is not yet completed, although we have had from one to five neighbor men working at different times with the building of frames and pouring of cement. Even I have helped by cooking for the men, nailing laths, and driving to town with pickup and trailer for extra cement and sand.

October 15 No Hunting

Pheasants, quails, partridges, ducks, and geese are usually so plentiful in this county that no wild-fowl hunter should come home at evening empty handed. In the valleys there are plenty of natural covers for nesting: river marshes, orchards, roadside bushes, thicketed ravines threading up into the hills. Grain fields attract flocks of ducks and geese coming south in the autumn. Our mountainous end of the county should be a birds' paradise, with its moderate summer climate; abundant supply of wild seeds, insects, water; and thousand of acres of brushy land ideal for hiding nests. No matter where one rides into the hills, there is always a bird singing for anyone who listens. Some birds seem to like human companionship, because they are more prevalent in the trees around the homes and orchards than in trees farther back in the hills.

The first winter we were here, the extreme cold and deep snow nearly wiped out the quail and pheasant population on our ranch. Feeling that these few remaining little birds needed protection and were also our best natural protection from insects, we decided to tack up NO HUNTING signs along the road to save the birds, as well as our cattle and hogs. Since then we have abandoned the plan, because we found that the hunters paid absolutely no attention to the signs. My laying hens cackle and fly when a shot rings out across the thicket from them. I am also frightened when a bullet whines over the garden, and feel that some people are very inconsiderate to come in so close to farm homes to do their shooting.

October 30 Blue's Foot

We searched high and we searched low, we searched up the creek and down the creek, across the creek and over the hills; we whistled and we called, but Blue pup had disappeared. We speculated on whether he had been run over, shot, poisoned, drowned, stolen, or pulled into a badger hole.

Six days later, after we had given up hope of finding him, he came limping home, dripping wet, and ravenously hungry. Across his front paw was the mark of a big trap—how cruel for a trapper to leave his traps unattended for so many days.

Day by day the little dog grew more ill as his toes, dead from no blood circulation, gradually dropped off. We made him a soft bed in the garage, warmed his food which he would hardly touch, and gave him shots of penicillin.

When the foot began to heal, he began feeling better, and can now hop around on three feet. But he will always be crippled, and the duty for which we raised him—driving cattle—is lost. If we were more hard-hearted, we would dispose of him and replace him with another pup; but if I know us, we will keep him until he dies of old age.

November 21 Golden Bananas

Large yellow and blue and pink banana squashes hidden here and there beneath their high green foliage are a thrill to the grower who has watched their magical expansion during summer days after the big flat seeds were deposited carefully in the warm May soil.

But the question is: What can a 4-H boy, who wants to make a little profit on his project, do with the produce when frost is coming. Town is miles away, stores will buy very few squashes, and little boys quake at the mere thought of peddling. Danny's father advised him to clear a place in the garage to store the squashes away from rain and frost, then to put a "Squashes For Sale" sign up by the road.

It wasn't a soft job, cutting away the big leaves and raspy vines, and loading and unloading a ton of big, hard-to-get-a-hold-of squashes into and out of the pickup. But, uncomplainingly, he completed the task and hung a set of scales in a handy place for weighing. His mother printed the cardboard sign which he nailed up by the mailbox.

He seriously doubted that anyone would bother to stop. Every evening when he arrived home from school he would ask, "Did anyone come for squashes today?" Now and then a neighbor or a hunter or a family from the valley did surprise us by stopping for a squash or two. By Thanksgiving, they were all sold and Dan had over $50 to show for his project work.

In August, he felt that he had been mis-advised when his mother insisted that he take three of his nicest squashes to the county fair for a 4-H exhibit. His brother Johnny had won prize money on his pigs and then brought them home; Jimmy had won a dollar on his electrification exhibit and brought it home; but he, Dan, had only won a dollar on first prize and the squashes were no good to bring home. Whereas, if he had left them at home on the vines, they would have matured and sold for three or four dollars!

November 30 Fruit—Row Upon Row

Just a minute before the first fall rain started to drop, we put the last nail in the last strip of roofing over our fruit cellar.

How convenient to walk down covered, concrete steps, without having to lift a heavy, flat door or shovel snow from its top. A light switch is handy when the stairway is dark; two bulbs within the cellar light up the big bin full of potatoes, the tub of carrots buried in sand, the bushel baskets of red and yellow apples, the meat brine barrel, the rows of white eggs in their crate, the big blue and yellow squashes stacked at one side, the white wax onions hanging in a mesh sack from a rafter, a box of sweet peppers and tomatoes gathered just before the frost to finish ripening, and rows of canned food in glass jars.

If, in some years, I have an overabundance of certain fruits or vegetables, and have enough spare time, I go ahead and can them; because, should the next year find them scarce or none at all from frost or insects, I will have a welcome supply carried over.

Inside a calendar on the cellar wall, I jot down the amount of each product canned during the season, as well as those carried over from the previous year; then, when the next planting and canning season begins, I check the jars on the shelves to see how much we have used during the last year and thereby gauge the needed amounts to can.

There are between four hundred and seven hundred quarts to record.

The list usually includes:

red raspberries	blackberry jam	sauerkraut
sweet cherries	pear preserves	mixed pickles
vegetable soup	dill pickles	prunes
tomato catsup	mince meat	pears
strawberry preserves	grape juice	pie cherries
cauliflower pickles	tomatoes	apricots
grape-apple jelly	grape jelly	plum jelly
green beans	apple butter	prune butter
black raspberries	plums	applesauce
pickled beets	rhubarb	peaches
tomato juice	blackberries	raspberry jelly
apricot butter	corn	watermelon preserves

Some vegetables, such as peas, green lima beans, greens, and cauliflower, we prefer to freeze and store in the locker. At the first glance, this list appears to be quite a variety, but actually it isn't, as anyone who examines a canning recipe booklet can tell you.

— YEAR OF 1953 —
MUD

January 11 Bookkeeping

This is the month of the year when all good farmers must bring forth all accounts of business transacted during the preceding year and transcribe the results onto the new income tax forms. And woe unto the one who hasn't kept records!

The urgent and annoying question is: Exactly how many gallons of gas did we use, how much did it cost, and did we use any of it for pleasure? Did I forget to add in the value of those eggs I traded to Mrs. Neighbor for wheat? Did we buy or raise that old cow we sold, and could she be termed a breeder for capital investment, did we depreciate her, and, let's see now, was it August 5 when we took her to the sale, or was it September 10, and in what year did we buy her? Do I show loss or profit on the old hayrake that we traded in for the new one, and how many years shall I decide to take for depreciation on the new rake? How much "hidden" interest did we pay on that note? Around and around it goes and who knows?

The records we kept the first year that we were here on the ranch didn't match the data called for in the income tax forms—veterinary supplies had to be separated from feed costs, supplies from maintenance, and, in fact so many such figures had to be re-added and re-subtracted that we wondered if we ever would get it straightened out. Clark still wishes for an adding machine.

The second year we purchased a little farm record book, based on the entries on the income tax listings, and thereby cut down on the numerical work.

The third year our bank sent us a record book having a page for each entry of the income tax papers. This method simplified the bookkeeping so much for that year, that I decided to accept the plan permanently, but could find no similar record books for sale. Therefore, we bought a post binder in which to make our own entry arrangement, and it will also be convenient to have all of the years' records in one book for ready reference.

When anyone in the family digs a receipt or bill from his pocket, he slips it into the pocket of the calendar by the door. Later, when I enter the amounts in the book, I transfer the slips of papers to another monthly file for future evidence.

I wonder how many farmers have to keep their business papers and writing supplies scattered around in shelves, drawers, cardboard boxes, and trunks, as we do. I hope we are the only ones.

My fondest dream of a home business center is an enormous, old-fashioned, roll-top desk with dozens of cubby holes and drawers in which to file within fingertip reach such items as envelopes, stationery, postcards, stamps, pens, blotters, pencils, ink, answered and unanswered letters, bills to be paid, bank statements, account books, addresses, equipment instructions and guarantees, gasoline records, income tax copies, insurance papers, safe-deposit box, receipts, manuscripts. May it also be large enough for a comfortable writing counter and accessories, as a lamp, calendar, dictionary, and typewriter.

You ask, "Why the old roll-top?" That is for the purpose of safeguarding all papers when I am suddenly called away from the desk. I can quickly pull the top down, and if I don't find time to get back to the desk for a week or two, the papers will still be waiting with no disturbance. Or if I have only a few moments here and there between tasks, I can spend them in writing, rather than in hunting and putting away papers.

January 18 Hemorrhagic

When we gathered in our cattle before Christmas, we found a calf dead, and some of the others didn't look too well, but we thought the drought of last fall which prevented new grass growth had left the cattle in poor condition for the winter. However, soon after the calves were weaned and put into the feed lot, another one died with the symptoms of hemorrhagic septicemia.

Immediately, we rushed to town for vaccine and penicillin. Those that weren't too sick, we managed to save, but to this date, we have lost seven of those big spring calves.

Carcasses everywhere! Down in the bushes a weak old cow couldn't get up and died. A new-born calf died. Babe, our gentle, faithful, old work mare got down in the mud in the corral and was too weak to rise, so Clark had the piteous task of shooting her.

January 20 Impaled

In the mornings, after Clark loads the hay onto the wagon, I have been going with him to drive the tractor while he throws the hay off to the cattle on the sand bars along the creek where there isn't much mud. I don't like driving with the big-tined fork sticking threateningly out in front, but Clark leaves it attached to use when loading the hay from the stack. I try to carefully watch the tines so that they won't catch on anything as we weave slowly in and out among the willows and cows.

This morning we were nearly unloaded and ready to re-cross the creek, when Doog, the big dog that is half collie and half Chesapeake Bay retriever, decided to give chase to a cow that was slow in crossing. In the cow's excitement, she ran around the front of the tractor. I was trying to call the dog back and hadn't noticed that the tines were lowered to a dangerous level. I wasn't used to the hand clutch on this new tractor, and, though I desperately needed to stop, I couldn't remember quickly enough which instrument to push or to pull! Suddenly the cow stopped—impaled on a corner tine.

"Stop, you've killed a cow!" Clark yelled.

The tractor was stopped but I didn't know where to shift into the reverse gear, nor what to do, so I scrambled down off the seat and chased the dog away while Clark jumped onto the tractor and slowly backed away from the cow. I held my breath, expecting to see her fall over dead; but instead, she walked away and started eating hay!

Several times during the day we have gone down to see if she is dead but she seems to be all right. The tine ran in full length in front of her hip bone where, evidently, it didn't puncture any vital organ.

January 22 Perfumed

We stirred and dissolved obnoxious smelling poisonous insecticide powder in buckets of water and dumped it into the 100 gallons of water in the tank of a rented sprayer that was mounted on a truck.

After the balky sprayer motor finally started, we pointed the long rubber hose at the cattle milling around in the pole corral; when the spray struck them, they humped in a bunch as though a wild storm had descended upon them.

Although we didn't want to breathe the spray or get it on us, we had to keep those white-faces moving around so that the force of the spray could penetrate through their hair on all sides. We ran this way and that, yelling and prodding at them to keep them shifting until the spray was all used up and the cattle dripping wet.

I guess no lice or other insects will bother that herd for awhile; in fact, I think I am safe, too.

April 5 No Telephone?

Sometimes a telephone would be most welcome.

After supper a young man came to the door to see if we could let him have a tire for his car, as he had had a blowout and no spare. Clark told him that we didn't have any that would fit his car. The fellow said he had to get to town to make an important telephone call, so Clark offered to take him back to a service station up-valley.

While there, Clark learned (in an aside from the storekeeper) that the man was taking his wife to the hospital to have a baby! Needless to say, no more time was lost in coming back and getting the tire ready to go. Thank goodness, I knew nothing about it, or I most certainly would have been pacing the floor, worrying if I could cope with such an emergency.

We still had a little time left to get ready to go to the Farm Bureau meeting in town. I wrapped the big potato salad for the potluck supper and we were off.

We seemed to be a little early for the gathering, and a stranger came up to the car to ask if we had come to the meeting. When we said, "Yes," he introduced himself and said he was glad we had come. I thought, "This is rather strange." As chairwoman, I had tried to attend most of the meetings, and I thought I knew all of the local members. Perhaps another family from out of town had joined, or, rather, out of the local community?

We decided there was time enough to slip over to the telephone office to make a needed call, and while there, quite by accident, we learned that the Farm Bureau meeting had been postponed!

Another close call. How embarrassed would we have been, had we found us and our potato salad sitting in at a private meeting of another organization! We quickly headed home, glad that we had eaten earlier and not put our trust in potluck.

Had we had a telephone, perhaps we would have been notified of the postponed meeting.

April 20 Woodcraft

This morning Jimmy wandered off, saw in hand, in search of an ancient sagebrush with which to form a table lamp. It is surprising what a twelve-year-old boy can do with a shaggy, old limb from a sagebrush (especially when he has his right arm in a sling, having just had the cast removed from a fractured elbow which, as yet, he can only straighten to a right angle!). After hours of whittling with a pocket knife, smoothing with sandpaper, and shellacking, the gnarled piece became an individual work of art with its twisted curves and dimples reflecting the different shades of browns and tans. It promises to be a ranch house natural when it is completed. For the base he may decide to use driftwood if he can find an acceptable piece along the creek.

Dan has completed an unusual set of book ends by sawing two crotched pieces from four-inch-in-diameter pine limbs. He whittled off the bark and smoothed the wood, leaving just enough roughness for a rustic effect under the shellac. On the top ends, which were sawed at a slant, he burned our two cattle brands—the bar A bar and the open A lazy L.

April 21 Country Art

As Clark was going to drive ten miles up the valley to do a few hours welding for a neighbor, I decided to ride along to visit with the neighbor's wife, take her some early green onions, and find if she was ready for the raspberry plants I have been saving for her. However, my visit was cancelled when on the road we met the neighbor, who told us that his wife was attending a textile painting class at another neighbor's home.

I decided to visit the class. Eight ranch women were sitting around tables, busily tracing patterns, blending colors, and painting flowers on pillow cases. All but three of these women have small children. I listened to them talking about how each had spent the morning—they had helped to drive cattle, or clean the chicken house, or plant garden, or drive the school bus—this I knew was in addition to all of their regular house work, outdoor chores, getting the children off to school, and preparing the noon meal.

What determination, thought I, to learn this work of beauty, when it would have been so much easier to have taken a nap in the afternoon with the babies. This was their third lesson—one lesson a week—seven more weeks to go, right at the busiest season.

June 20 Bundles of Hay

Suddenly the sun is shining! After so many days of rain and ranchers' scowls, the weather has turned perfect and everybody is rushing to make hay while the sun shines. Again we are using another method. We have purchased one of the new model, small hay balers which ejects neat bundles of firmly packed, green colored hay as it eats and chops its way around the fields of windrowed alfalfa.

How well it operates depends to a great extent on the operator who watches and adjusts it as he pulls it around with the tractor. Some people have shook their heads and doubted that the three boys (ages twelve, fourteen, and sixteen) could learn to run the baler and put up the hay alone; but Clark, believing that they can do it, has gone to work in the woods.

My worry isn't so much that they will fail to grease or run the machines properly, as that they may forget to be careful of the dangerously powered equipment.

August 15 Red Blackberries Are Green

"I wouldn't do it, Mother! If I had to do all of that work just to get some blackberries to eat, I would simply go without."

By the time I had cut every weed from under the vines, tied or propped all hanging branches up away from the ground, and sprinkled the soil underneath with chlordane, I was beginning to think that Jimmy was right. One session of creeping around under the thorny vines doesn't complete the job, either—the weeds keep growing, the vines are blown off their props or fall with weight as they grow, and the chlordane dust must be applied after each weekly irrigation to ward off the earwigs. Blackberries ripen over a period of weeks and should be picked every two or three days. The stickery branches cling to clothing and skin with the tenacity of cats' claws, so that scratches on hands and arms never get healed from one picking to the next; needles and tweezers are kept in a convenient place for the removal of inevitable briars broken off in the flesh of the fingers.

Early in the spring, we had pruned off the tops of the three rows of blackberries and raspberries, and also removed old dried-up canes and excess growth. All this cut-off debris had to be raked up and carried over to the bare garden to be burned. Previously, we had driven posts and attached wire to hold the black raspberries from falling over, and I had hauled manure out of the hen house (in the little red wagon) and spread it around the vines. This fertilization also makes the weeds grow rampantly, some reaching the height of ten feet when we don't find time to cut them.

But, somehow, when I walk into the house in the morning with two buckets full of big, luscious, shiny, blackberries, I forget about all the toil involved.

August 17 This Way or That?

The weather remained perfect for haying and the boys completed the stacking of 150 tons of hay without any serious accidents, thank goodness. Of course, Clark helped them on weekends and evenings whenever they had a serious or major machinery breakdown. Even so, they couldn't have done it without the baler, as the hay would have had to have been stacked more promptly. The hardest work of all was gathering the fifty pound bales from the fields into big loads on the trucks and trailers and hauling them home to stack.

As none of us had ever had experience in stacking baled hay, we sought advice from neighbors, but still found it a difficult task to arrange the bundles this way and that way to make them fit snugly into a rectangular form without allowing any sides or corners to be loose, slant in, or bulge out. The derrick was used to hoist the bales up onto the big stack; smooth wire was attached to corner poles and a few pieces of wire netting were laid between the layers of hay to help keep them from sliding out.

The stacks look substantial enough to withstand the winter weather; and the boys are quite proud of their completed assignment.

August 30 No First Aid?

"Mother! Mother! Come here quick. Dan's got creosote dip in his eyes!" Jim shouted. I hastily set the berry bucket down and dashed past the thorny bushes up to the house. Dan had his head over the sink where he was dousing his face with cold water.

"Do something quick! My eyes are burning up! Quick, do something!"

No doubt something did need to be done and done immediately. Water alone was not effective. There was eye salve in the medicine cabinet but I doubted if it would do any good. Grabbing a towel and an egg and a cup from the cupboard, I ordered Dan to lie down on the cot while I broke the egg into the cup and framed the towel around his face. Then I poured the albumen into his eyes, and almost instantly the burning ceased.

"How did you get creosote into your eyes?" I asked.

"It isn't creosote," he explained. "It's post treat—pentachlorophenol mixed with stove oil. I was pouring some out of the barrel, and, when I let it set back down, it sloshed out right into my eyes!"

"Well, you can be thankful it was diluted with oil," I told him. "Now get your shirt off. I'll put some hot water and detergent into the tub, and we'll see if we can scrub it off of your skin before it blisters."

We found that it took more than one handful of strong detergent and tub of water to cut into that stove oil and remove it from his hair. When he appeared to have no traces left except the odor, we dried him and again applied albumen to his eyes.

Since then I have wondered about the adequacy of our medicine cabinet. A family living four miles from the nearest telephone and twenty-five miles from a doctor or hospital should be prepared for emergencies. I have checked this list of supplies in our cabinet:

iodine	absorbent cotton	cough medicine
lysol	adhesive tape	rubbing alcohol
nose drops	burn ointment	eucalyptus oil

tweezers	merthiolate	powdered alum
needles	mercurochrome	hydrogen peroxide
resinol	carbolic acid	mosquito repellant
lip salve	petroleum jelly	scissors
camphor	calamine lotion	hot water bottle
musterole	milk of magnesia	thermometer
liniment	epsom salts	tongue depressors and swabs
tannic acid	ear drops	Red Cross first aid book
eye salve	caster oil	bicarbonate powder
zinc powder	aspirin tablets	tincture of green soap

It hardly seems possible that we would ever use all of these items, yet sooner or later each one fills a special need, either at the house or barn.

Still, I can see that there are several things missing—a poison antidote, gauze bandages, rattlesnake kit, and perhaps the most needful of all—a course in first aid treatment. What good will a book do if someone needs artificial respiration? Why was I not taught these emergency aids? Why aren't all children required to know first aid before they are allowed to graduate from the elementary grades? Why teach them the names of all the bones in the body, but not how to make a splint for one? Very few people ever live this far from a doctor; never-the-less, there are millions of times when trained hands could quickly aid accident victims and save lives before the doctor's arrival.

If only raw eggs were the solution to everything.

September 5 Sale Day

This year the duty fell upon my and the boys' shoulders to go with the yearling cattle to the sale ring. When the last cattle truck pulled away from the corral, we climbed into the car to follow; that is, all except Jimmy, who doesn't like sales and decided to remain at home.

I wished that I could have stayed at home, too. There was the inevitable argument with the brand inspector over a brand which had grown crooked on a holstein dairy calf. Then came the long wait, sitting on hard plank seats inside the sales building, while animal after animal was whipped and driven around and through the pavilion and onto the big scales. The auctioneer's quick, mumbled, bid-calling voice was shouted continually through the loud speaker to contend with the shrieking hogs, bawling cattle, and baaing sheep.

Below us, behind us, on all sides of us sat listening stockmen and buyers. The cattlemen are usually easy to distinguish from the valley farmers by their attire of Stetsons, Levis, leather or wool jackets, cowboy boots, sport or cowboy style shirts, shirt pockets stuffed full of billfolds, checkbooks, and pens; while the farmers mostly wear heavy work shoes, waist or bib overalls, chambray shirts, caps or work-type straw hats. But from mountain or valley, they all smoked cigarettes or cigars until I sometimes thought I couldn't wait until I could run outside for a breath of fresh air. A few sullen looking women sat here and there, either accompanying their husbands or waiting for their pigs or cows to be sold, so that they could call for their checks and be on their way to pay off a few bills.

When at last our cattle started coming in from the holding pens, I checked the identity and selling price of each on paper for our own records. After the last one was run onto the scales, we waited at the office for the check, with which I knew Clark would be disappointed. Then at town we loaded up some feed and supplies and headed back toward the mountains.

It was a little late when we reached home, and I wondered why Jimmy didn't have the milk cows in the barn yard. I thought he must be having trouble in finding them; then I noticed the saddle horse in the corral and wondered why he hadn't ridden him. Within a few minutes Dan drove the cows in, and said that Jimmy was no place in sight. I began to feel alarmed. Where in the world was he? I told Johnny to drive the car up the road each way, from where he could look down into the fields. I called. I looked in the attic, in the cellar, in the shop, down by the creek where it was possible he might have gone to sleep on the sand. Surely he wouldn't have gone alone down to the deep swimming hole two miles away in the canyon.

When Johnny came back, he said, "I didn't see him any place. He said something this morning about taking the caterpillar tractor down and pulling out those big locust trees. . . ." (I could see him lying on that tractor with a massive tree on top of him.) "But," Johnny continued, "the cat is down by the creek right where I left it."

Surely if he had gone off in a car with anyone he would have left a note. It was barely possible that Clark had been laid off from work for the afternoon and come home, then gone some other place, taking Jimmy with him. There was nothing to do now but pace the floor, get supper, and wait for Clark.

When I saw the pickup coming down the road from the direction of the timber, I thought, "No, he hasn't been home." I ran out to the gate to meet him, and *there* on the seat beside him was Jimmy.

"Sonny," I began, "I've been worried to death. Why in the wide world did you go off without leaving a note?"

Clark stopped me, "Just a minute, don't say any more. Some man came here this afternoon and scared him off."

When things had quieted down enough to get the story, here is what it was: In the afternoon a man had come walking down the driveway. Now, we live so far from town and neighbors that no one ever comes walking in unless he has had car trouble or run out of gas. But such things didn't seem to be this man's trouble. He wanted to know where Jimmy's mother and father were. When Jimmy told him, he then wanted to know what kind of cars they were driving and exactly what time they were expected home. Jimmy gave him the details and then wanted to know if he had any message that he wanted to leave. "No," the man said, "I will be back to see them later," and went walking back up the driveway.

Jimmy, not liking the looks of the man's disheveled clothing and unkept hair, put the lock on the gas tank as soon as he was out of sight. At about that time, the sound of a car door slamming shut, down around the bend, sent Jimmy running toward the barn to hide. Sure enough, an old green car pulled into the driveway and honked its horn. When Jimmy didn't come running out, the man yelled, "Is anybody home?"; and when no one answered, he started toward the house. Jimmy heard the screen door slam and knew that the man had gone inside. Soon he came out and, through a crack between the barn siding, Jimmy could see him starting for the barn.

Not waiting another second, Jimmy darted out the back of the barn, past the haystack, down the hill, and up the creek through the brush, never stopping to remove his shoes when he waded the water, or to worry about getting sunburned without a shirt. Afraid the dog might reveal any hiding place he could find, he hurried along for four miles over rocky hills and through brush before he decided to stop at a neighbor's home and wait until time for his father to come home from work.

The neighbors were bewildered at such strange doing, but not a word could they get from the boy that anything amiss or unusual had happened. At about the time he figured his father would be coming along the road, Jimmy walked up to wait for him. When Clark heard the story he was frightened, because the desperado might still be at the ranch; and, with no forewarning, the boys and I would arrive before he did. Consequently, he was as relieved to find us safe as we were to find Jimmy.

We didn't discover any guns or food or gas or anything else missing that an outlaw might want. I guess we will never know whether Jimmy had been listening to too many radio crime stories, or if the man actually was a bad character. But of one thing I am quite sure: Jimmy will accompany us to the sales from now on.

September 28 Cat at Work

Almost every year we have to have some conservation work done in the creek to stabilize the banks and keep high water from washing away good soil.

This year I was unbelieving when Clark said that, in order to save some money, we could rent a Caterpillar tractor from a neighbor, and

Johnny could do the work on weekends after school started, and the water was low.

I thought, "How in the world can he work that huge machine, when I doubt if he has ever been on one before, doesn't know how to start it, and no one will be here to instruct him on the work!"

But they went right ahead with their plans. What boy doesn't dream of operating one of those big, powerful, noisy, diesel-eating machines? Not wanting any part of a mixup like that, I stayed entirely away from the project, only praying that he wouldn't upset the rig.

Reports kept coming in of work hours mounting up, sand bars disappearing, boulders and brush being pushed up onto banks for channel control, little fields being bulldozed free of thorn and willow trees.

The work is completed now, and I must admit that it was a triumph of boy and engine power over the ravages of nature.

September 30 — Zeros and Crosses

I was surprised when a woman who has lived for sixty years told me that she had never painted anything. It seems that everyone should have had the delight of painting something during their lifetime. Perhaps not all have the talent for painting pictures, but how about a house, or a rose trellis, or some chairs, or even flower pots?

This time, in my case, it has been linoleum. About once a year, before or after the main summer work, I come home from town with two or three cans of paint, and await a warm day when everyone else is away from home. I paint only half of the kitchen floor this first day, because we have to use the range and table on the other half while the first part is drying.

The following morning, when the paint on the first half has dried, I make a design over it with different colored paints and a smaller brush. This pattern may be as original as I like, as long as it isn't too hard to apply. In days past there have been various sized half moons, the Bar A Bar cattle brand, dashes running at right angles to each other, splatters made with a scrub brush, woven tread pressed on with a mesh onion sack, and, this time, a black-board game of zeros and crosses.

The third morning I move the table and chairs back onto the newly painted part and start on the second half. As we have to come through the door and use the sink on this side, I must find a long board to place on little blocks over the wet paint to form a walk for the night. The fourth night the board path must be used again. On the fifth morning everyone is relieved to again be allowed to step anywhere on the floor.

This time they weren't so pleased when they come home on the fifth evening to find the woodwork on one side of the kitchen glistening wet with white paint.

"Oooooooh," they groaned, "We gotta go through all this again?"

"Yes, and I must paint only part of it at a time or we would be sure to get our clothes against it someplace," I cheerily reply.

Clark adds, "Gosh, if this painting lasts for a month, I don't believe I can stand it."

I pretended to laugh gleefully at their annoyed expressions and go on to tease, "Oh, now, perk up. Don't get tired yet, as I am thinking of doing the other end of the house before I quit."

But to myself I think, "Doubt if I could stand it either!"

October 19 Big Game Hunters

Danny and Johnny were up early in the cold morning and eagerly starting out afoot before daylight with their red caps and rifles.

Johnny had borrowed his Dad's red hunting cap and old, long-barreled 25-35 Winchester. I had pinned a red handkerchief over the top of Dan's old cap, and he was proudly carrying the brand new 30-30 Winchester rifle. Since this was the first year we had felt that Dan was old enough to carry a big rifle, his Dad had purchased the rifle so the two boys could go hunting together. In their pockets, the boys carried matches and bullets and hunting licenses and tags; on their belts were sacked lunches and big hunting knives.

I didn't hear any shots all day, and, close to supper time I was just beginning to feel a little bit anxious for their return when suddenly Johnny came walking in alone to announce, "Dan shot a big doe up over the hill about a mile away. I can't take time to eat supper; I've got to take Prince back to load the deer on and get it packed in before dark."

We were surprised to learn that Dan had had such good luck on his very first day out with the new rifle. Supper was postponed for several hours while Clark went back with Johnny to help and show them how to load the deer and tie it securely onto the saddle to get it home over the steep hills.

They were two mighty tired boys by the time the venison was skinned and cleaned and hung up in the locust tree to cool during the night. They had tramped all day over rough, rocky hills and through brushy draws, seeing many deer tracks but no deer, until, on their way home, they had startled the doe from a willow thicket.

October 30 Wind(y) Falls

After taking salt to the cattle on The Eighty, Clark and I decided to drive another mile back into the hills to a place that had belonged to my grandfather and grandmother in the late pioneer days. At that time, in the early nineteen hundreds, the farmstead had been a bower of beauty, nestled below springs, within tossing distance of the tiny, pure-water stream, and protected from early frosts by the encircling sage hills. The white, six-room house had been homey and comfortable. But, while the rooms were then modern with flowery wallpaper, had woven and plush carpets, organ, stereoscope, pieced and embroidered velvet quilts over featherbeds, lounge, settee, wash basins with accompanying water pitchers, wood-burning stoves, hand-pumped water, family picture albums, and rocking chairs with feather cushions, the real beauty lay in the outside surroundings of carefully placed plantings.

Between the house and the hillside cut, into which it had been foundationed, ran a wooden walk overhung with a profusion of roses and apple tree boughs. To the west, blue irises, red and pink and yellow roses, cherry and plum and almond trees bordered one side of the croquet court. Below the house, wooden steps led down to the fruit cellar and the spring house from which cold water poured past the black walnut and cedar trees to nourish the apple and peach orchard and vegetable garden which ended in the wild thickets of the creek. The morning sun shone over the barnyard, catalpa bordered pond, and hillside peach orchard before filtering through the black locust leaves onto the white walls of the bungalow.

Now the ponds are dry. The buildings are gone. Nothing is left but a few, old, gnarled fruit and nut trees, and the spring water running into a watering trough and on to the brook. The former green alfalfa fields have been turned into dry grazing land. A few white-face cows trot down to nab the wormy apples as they fall to the ground.

I had lived here as a child, picked the roses, climbed the apple trees, cracked walnuts in the attic, fished in the little stream, ran barefoot up the paths in summer, played house in the orchards with neighborhood children. Now there are no neighbors, no school house. All of the homes close by have been abandoned. The small homestead standard of living is a memory.

We tasted some of the apples and found them so surprisingly delicious that we decided to take a few home with us in a burlap sack. We filled the sack, and then tasted apples from other trees which were even more delicious. We couldn't bear to let them go to waste, so we started pouring them into the back of the car until they were level with the seat; then added two sacks full of black walnuts.

Not having a ladder, we had to shake most of the apples down from the limbs and chase them down the hill—like left fielders trying to catch three grounders at once, and also keep from getting hit on their heads at the same time!

November 12 — Papering Hay

"Housewife" isn't the proper title for a woman on a ranch. It should be "Ranchwife." No two days work are the same, nor are they often completed within the house.

This morning instead of baking the gingerbread, I was pressed into duty at the barn to help figure out how to cover the high haystack with paper. You wonder why "paper"? Well, it was rolls of tough, flexible, waterproof paper to keep the rains and melting snows from soaking down into the bales of hay causing spoilage.

We measured the stack and measured the paper and cut off proper lengths and toted them up the long, steep ladder to the top of the stack. (I stood below and gave instructions ?? and warnings about not getting too close to the edge of the stack, where a slip would have been perilous.)

They would get a piece of paper, or rather, a long strip, nearly in place and ready to anchor on the sides, when a gust of wind would come along and billow it up into the air like a circus tent on a windy day. Finally, by carrying bales of straw to weight them down, they got all of the strips overlapping in the correct places and tied down. Over the winter, I wondered which will come out the victor—paper or wind?

November 13 No Cider?

Did anyone surmise what happened to all of those bruised apples?

apple pie	apples to pare
apple cobbler	apples to quarter
baked apples	apples to slice
apple salad	apple leather
apples in lunches	apples in big kettles
apples in cellar	apples in jars
apple butter	apples in baskets
apple sauce	wormy apples

An apple a day—that's for sure. (Just try writing the word "apple" a few dozen times and see how queer it looks!)

November 19 Loading Chute

I'm glad that Clark is getting the new loading chute built into the corral—not that I enjoy going out into the frosty morning air to help hold the timbers in place with aching fingers while he drills holes and places bolts and nails, but because we need a facility for loading cattle into trucks and trailers. It scares me frantic to have to help get roped cows and bulls into vehicles.

Not long ago a neighbor came to get one of his heifers that had strayed in with our herd. Clark wasn't home, so I told the man to go ahead and use our old saddle horse to cross the creek and fetch the heifer.

He was gone a long time and, when he finally returned, he was almost dragging the stubborn heifer with a rope around its neck, and the old horse was dripping with sweat. The man managed to get the end of the rope fastened to his stock trailer, but the heifer would get no closer. She dodged this way and that way, and pulled back, and in her wild frenzy would chase any moving thing within sight and reach. Finally she choked herself onto the ground and the man had to loosen the rope so that she could regain consciousness.

I went out with a long stick (and an eye on a get-away place between trailer and pickup, should the lariat break) thinking perhaps I could heckle her from behind, while he pulled on the rope. This had no effect what-so-ever. At last the rancher took off his sombrero and waved it in her face. This made her so completely mad, that, with a "Baaow," she charged straight at him, not noticing that she was jumping into the trailer. My heart stood still until I saw the cowboy leap up and out over the front of the trailer, where he quickly took up the slack in the rope so that she couldn't back out.

I don't know which was most tired of the three—man, horse, cow—but, without a doubt, I was the most frightened!

I am hoping the new loading chute will alleviate some of this kind of energy loss and dangerous exhibitions.

— YEAR OF 1954 —
GREEN TOMATO SUMMER

January 18 Fine Winter

This has been a wonderfully mild winter, so different from others we have had in the past. The thermometer here hasn't even reached zero, and hollyhock leaves, where they have been protected by the side of the house, have remained green all winter.

Our cattle feeding, too, has changed. No more struggling all the day through snow, water, ice, and mud to reach and feed the white-faces. Our hay is stacked right here within easy reach of tractor and trailer. The new feed lot for the range cattle fences them in above the highway, where they have access to the moderate spring water and are kept away from the menacing ice and high water of the creek.

Now I no longer need to help with the feeding. Morning and evening, Clark and one of the boys throw some bales onto the trailer and haul them up to the long feed rack. In this way the cattle aren't fed too much at once, can't waste the hay by walking on it, and eat every tiny leaf that falls from the stems. The cut hay is so tightly packed into the bales that it is much easier to handle and feed than the long, loose hay.

Even the weaner calves are easier to feed, as the fence of their lot has been extended up onto the hill, where the feed racks form the side of it, close to the driveway. No gates to open or calves to shoo out of the way or hill to get stuck on—just drive along the outside of the pen and toss the cut bundles over the fence into the feed racks. Nor do we have the wet, icy job of hauling creek water to the calves, for now they sip warmer water out of an open tank filled by means of hoses from the faucet of the pressure pump line.

January 20 Wish Book

When I walked up to the road to get the mailsack, I thought, "What a lovely day for January." The sun was bright, the air clear, and there was the sound of rocks rolling down yonder mountain, loosened by last night's frost and this morning's sunshine. The yearling calves' white faces were lined up along the feeder where they were crunching good-smelling, green alfalfa hay; other calves were lazily basking in the warm, welcome sunshine.

There are more birds here now than there were a month ago. A frequent burst of song came from sparrows flitting restlessly from bare limb to bare limb of thorn and chokecherry thickets. I was fascinated, as usual, by a group of twittering juncos industriously scratching for food under rotted leaves in the yard. They do not scratch like chickens, first with one foot then the other, but they jump backward with both feet at the same time while raking leaves with their toenails.

In the mailsack I found a big spring-and-summer Sears Roebuck catalogue. Rather early, it seemed to me, but maybe we need some time to study on the latest of everything. I don't know what we would do without these merchandising dictionaries to keep us informed on prices and the newest of articles and styles!

We seldom go to town to shop and, when we do go, we haven't much time for looking around and comparing things. We must know approximately what we want and need, and the price we should pay for it. So, actually, we use the catalogues more for information than for ordering; although, many times we have shopped in Boise all day without finding the articles we wanted, then have come home to order them from the catalogue's wider selection.

Clark says I never look at any of the important things, such as tires and tools!

February 3 New Cook

Although it was quite a task, the boys didn't complain about having to do all of the chores while I was away at the hospital. On the days when Clark was also away with me, they had to rise early enough to milk eight cows, feed 100 head of range cows and calves, feed the pigs, haul the milk cans out to the road, cook and eat breakfast, wash their necks and change clothes before bus time at 7:30 a.m.

Jimmy accepted the job of cooking breakfast and supper, making and packing lunches, washing dishes, sweeping, and getting in the wood.

Here are the instructions that I left on the little blackboard:

BE SURE

1. The heater stove, electric range, lights, and radio are turned off.
2. The cat is out.
3. The chickens are fed and watered.
4. The calves are watered.
5. The door is shut well.

What more could I do, but pray? Nothing, it seemed, so I refused to worry; and the boys appeared to manage everything harmoniously.

I am glad they get along well together, for there isn't time nor room for arguing or fighting or teasing.

Sometimes Clark will come in for supper and say, "Those boys aren't hurrying a bit with their chores. They are just out there visiting."

Then I reply, "Well, be glad that they *are* visiting instead of fighting."

March 30 Rhizoma

Whether all seed drills have that deficiency or not, I do not know; but in all that we have rented or borrowed, the grass and legume seeds would never feed evenly down through the chutes. Which means that I have to ride on a board step behind the machine, wielding a stick, and poking here and there at the tiny seeds, while Clark drives the tractor. The dust rolls up around us, as I step precariously this way and that on the jittery moving drill, hang on with one hand, try to keep an eye on each bin of grass and alfalfa seed, as well as the open bin lids (which might bounce off balance and crack my fingers).

I had to be especially careful with what we planted today because it cost $12.50 for five pounds of seed. Clark wants to experiment with this new variety, which propagates itself by means of branching rhizomes, to see if it will make good grazing pasture on the newly-cleared bottom land.

April 7 By the Light of the Moon

We had eaten an early lunch so that Clark wouldn't have to return from the field until evening; and I, having worked hard all morning with cleaning and putting out a huge washing of clothes, had planned to relax a bit in the afternoon, read the newspaper, and perhaps take a nap.

But what usually happens to a ranchwife's plans? Here came Clark walking back. The tractor and digger harrow were stuck deep within the muck of the creek, and would I please go down with him to see if we could pull it out with the pickup?

The yellow violets and wild currants were in bloom; but I didn't have much time to enjoy them, what with block and tackle and more block and tackle strung out between mired tractor, thorn trees, and pickup, and signals to "Let 'er go!" After several attempts and "killing" of motors and loading pickup with rocks for weight traction and disconnection of harrow, out the tractor crawled, slopping water and sandy silt onto higher ground. Boy, what a lovely sight!

When I got back to the house, I couldn't relax, didn't have time for the nap, and to add to my harassment, the mail carrier didn't leave our mail—no paper to read.

Later in the afternoon Clark came in to suggest, "The weather is nice—let's get those wieners out of the freezer and have a wiener roast tonight." I agreed that this would be a pleasant evening for it—what with school spring vacation coming up tomorrow, and thirty calves to run through their marking ordeal and drive to pasture.

When evening approached, the boys built a huge bonfire with driftwood on a sandy spot on the center of the willow grove below the barn.

Just as the juice was beginning to drop into the flames from the fat wieners at the ends of our sharpened willow sticks, we heard several "ker plunks" over in the creek water. I thought someone was dropping rocks to scare us, but the boys said, "Hear that beaver splashing!" We turned to look and, sure enough, we caught a glimpse of him swimming close to the edge of the water on the far side of the creek. He pulled himself up onto the bank, chewed on a barky limb, then slid down his slick, muddy slide into the water again.

"Look, he's swimming over this way!" someone said. Hastily, we dashed the mustard and catsup onto our hot dogs, grabbed our plates of potato salad, and sneaked over to the creek edge. Mr. Beaver, with only his head sticking out of the water, swam to our side, then proceeded right on by us upstream.

Clark walked noisily over the gravel and stones to the very edge of the water, and we thought, "Oh, oh, this will scare him away." Instead, he calmly climbed up onto a rock, his brown, glossy fur dripping water, and sat there looking us over. Then with a gracious dive, he disappeared beneath the water and soon emerged again over by his slide.

I had no idea that beavers were so large—he must have weighed forty pounds. However, Dan said, "That was only a small one! And if he had been scared of us, he would have made a warning splash—that flat, bare tail of his hitting the surface of the water with a 'CRACK' like the sound of a rifle."

While the stars and bright new moon shone directly over us, we sat around the glowing embers, browning marshmallows, and telling the boys tales of picnics in the Model T and buggy days.

April 8 Open A Lazy L

Now that the boys are big enough to help, I try to stay away from the branding corral, until driving out time.

We have one or two improvements—instead of rubbing caustic around the tiny horns to stop their growth, we now use an electric dehorning iron which does a quicker, safer, and more efficient job. The old "Bar A Bar" brand on the right ribs has also been discarded for the "Open A Lazy L Connected" on the right hip. This new brand is easier to apply, grows better without running out of shape (less arguments with brand inspectors), and seems to heal more quickly on the hip where it is better protected from brush and flies.

April 16 Banquet vs. Pigs

While we were hurrying with the cow getting and feeding and milking, the horse watering, the shoe polishing, and other evening and "get ready" chores, so that we could get to the Future Farmer banquet on time, Dan came in with the news, "One of Johnny's sows is farrowing!"

We all looked at each other in bewilderment. What would we do now? Jimmy had been planning on going to the dinner for a week; Johnny was an officer in the organization, with a little speech to make, and also hoped to be presented with a special award; Danny was also a member, and this was his first banquet; Father and Mother were both expected to be present. But if Johnny neglected his project, and lost some of the pigs, he might be dubbed "Foolish Farmer" instead of Future Farmer.

Finally I said, "Jimmy, I know how much you want to go, but would you be willing to stay with Johnny's pigs?"

Johnny quickly added, "If he'll stay, I'll pay him a dollar an hour."

Jimmy looked quite crestfallen, but in a little while, after thinking it over, he overcame the disappointment and agreed to stay.

When we returned from the banquet at 11:00 p.m., we could hear the little radio playing at the barn; I half expected to find Jimmy asleep in the hay, but he came to meet us.

"Did she have any more pigs?" I asked.

He smiled and said, "What do you mean 'any more pigs'? She's got sixteen and they're every one alive!"

May 2 Asparagus Roots

Little did I dream of the work I was getting into when, last spring, I planted a pretty little packet of asparagus seeds. Almost every round seed sprouted and came up an inch apart to produce the daintiest of plumy foliage. Rejoicing over all of the fine asparagus plants I would have to set out the following spring, I sent to the U.S. Department of Agriculture for a bulletin on asparagus culture and studied exactly how to transplant the crowns; but I was surprised to learn that the roots might grow to be over ten feet in length!

Last week I decided the time was right to approach the plants with a shovel. A bushel basketful of barnyard manure went along to supply humus for the new sets. I quickly discovered, with the first shovelful lifted out, that I should have planted the seeds twelve inches apart instead of one. The bulletin had said, "Be careful not to injure the fleshy roots, as they are essential storage organs." And they weren't fooling when they mentioned "an extensive root system."

The pulpy roots weren't very long yet, but they resembled the strips of a cellulose sponge mop interwoven into freakish puzzles. "Be careful . . ." indeed! Lucky if I could untwine them by any means, gentle or otherwise. One shovelful yielded more plants than I could re-set in a half-hour. Soon my basketful of manure was used up and also the allotted space at the end of the strawberry and horseradish row.

In the two days following, I dug more holes; untwined more roots; dug more holes; carried more manure; dug more holes beside the cherry trees; dug more holes beside the pasture fence; dug more holes on the ditch bank; dug more holes; untwined more roots; dug more holes, until I "gave out"; and is the job completed? No! Half of the plants are still untouched! Now I'm beginning to wonder how those roots will look when digging time starts again next spring—ten feet long?!

May 6 Evening Grosbeaks

A queer, little cracking noise came from the direction of the thorn thicket. I was raking dry weeds at the lower end of the garden and wanted to finish burning the high tinder piles before supper time; but, since curiosity overcame my ambition, I walked closer to the trees to investigate. The sound subsided. No creature stirred as I peered around under the foliage and wondered if, perhaps, it could have been a porcupine chewing on a limb high overhead.

Suddenly, only a few feet from me, a flock of yellowish colored birds, slightly smaller than robins, descended from the limbs and started busily cracking seeds with their bills. Their tranquility astounded me as I studied the blackness of their bobbing tails and the snow white coverts of their black wings. When I observed the bright yellow crowns of their heads, I discovered why they could crack the hard thorn seeds—they had short, wide, super-strong bills.

Reluctantly, I turned back to the weed job, wishing that these colorful, friendly little fellows would stay as our guests all summer instead of only stopping to dine on their northward journey.

May 11 Rhubarb

Choice of three things to do this morning—wash rayon blouses, hoe in the garden, or ride Prince to the Lower Place to get some rhubarb. Not much doubt of the decision, is there?

The dogs were so happy to see me saddling the horse for a jaunt, but, when I mounted, poor old Laddie, knowing that he could no longer keep pace with the horse, sadly turned back to the house.

I would have enjoyed sitting all day in the knee-deep grass, cutting big rhubarb leaves from the shiny, pink stalks, listening to the red-winged blackbirds' warnings chirped from the boughs overhanging the rippling creek water, watching Prince crunch huge mouthfuls of grass, and laughing at Blue as he lifted puzzled ears toward the come-hither whistle of a bobwhite quail in the green grain fields.

Unwillingly, I pocketed my knife, boosted the two sacks full of rhubarb onto the saddle, and headed back toward the house for an afternoon of rhubarb canning.

The whole out-of-doors was ornate with white and yellow blossoms: the overly-sweet buckbrush, a few lingering violets and buttercups, hillside patches of balsam root, thorn tree blossoms, long clusters of white chokecherry blossoms looking like soft, little lambs' tails swaying in the breeze. If it hadn't been such a bother to climb off and onto the horse with the sacks of rhubarb, I would have picked a bouquet of the brightest yellow flowers of all—a cluster of ragwort growing alone in a dry gully.

May 30 Marauder?

It is possible that a good fur trapper could, within a radius of three miles from our cabin, take badger, skunk, civet cat, beaver, muskrat, black bear, coyote, lynx or bob cat, raccoon, weasel, mink, cottontail and jack rabbit.

Our natural history teachers tell us that the burrowing mammals are our friends because they fertilize, deepen, irrigate, loosen, and enrich the topsoil. However, this isn't the reason we have abstained from trapping—we just haven't had the extra time, and, anyway, trapping hasn't been a very profitable business lately. Until now our only trapping has been my endeavor to catch mice, and gophers in the garden. When carrot roots get gnawed off and irrigation water runs down holes, it is time for me to bring out the old box trap.

Thinking that the ground squirrels are getting entirely too numerous with their holes and mounds down in the pasture north of the barn, Dan hunted up some traps and set them when on his way to get the milk cows in the evenings. He was having good luck, in fact, had caught several dozen, before the dog began to get wise to the fun and raided the traps during the day. He also pulled the traps out and lost them (or at least Dan suspected him of all this), so Dan has discontinued his destruction of the "beneficial" burrowers.

June 1 Cat and Mouse

Six cuddly, baby kittens hidden in a warm nest of straw in the barn— I wonder if this is the climax to my cat story. Having had, at different times before in my life, to "get rid" of surplus kittens, I have consistently refused to allow a female cat upon our premises.

When we first arrived here there was a big, yellow tomcat, hiding out around the barn and bushes, that we soon gentled and sometimes brought into the house for food and warmth during the cold winter. The second spring someone, evidently thinking this was an easy dump, left a half-grown yellow cat with sore eyes. Before we realized that it was sick, the stray cat died, and soon we discovered that Big Yellow Tom had contracted the disease. We doctored his eyes, hoping to save him, but he grew thinner and thinner and finally crawled under the house and died.

It is really surprising how fast mice will increase within a few months. Cats either eat a vast number of them or else scare them away. Anyway, we had mice jumping out of grain buckets and cow stanchions in the barn, mice climbing onto the table in the separator room, mice leaping all ways and nearly falling onto our heads when we opened the granary door, mice chewing into boxes in the garage, mice slipping through holes and peeking at me from behind the mash feeder in the chicken house, mice making nests behind fruit jars in the cellar, mice eating kernels from stored popcorn in the top of the woodshed, mice stench permeating everything within the little room off the porch; but wonder of wonders, no mice inside the house! How did they know about those half-dozen new mouse traps. . . ?

Warfarin was just coming onto the market then, so we bought a couple of dollars worth to mix with ground corn. This preparation, which causes internal hemorrhages, isn't as dangerous to use as other poisons. It worked all right. Soon there were pieces of dead, fuzzy fur lying all around the place—in grain sacks and buckets and, especially, where a certain person put her hand in the dark cellar to find a jar of fruit!

Did this put an end to the mice? Uh uh! They kept right on converging on us. Finally, after weeks of inquiry, we found a friend who would let us have two male kittens, one black and one gray (if we hadn't wanted cats, probably everyone in the country would have had extra kittens for us). They were wild little creatures until they began to feel at home in the garage and to slip out in the evenings to scamper over the woodpile. When they grew large enough to go to the barn, the mice began to grow scarce.

One morning when the kittens were nearly grown, we found the black one dead on the garage floor. Since it hadn't been sick, my theory was that it had jumped for a sparrow in the loft, missed its footing, and broke its neck in falling. Of course, the boys didn't agree with this, as they said that cats always land on their feet.

By now we have grown quite attached to Gray Tommy, who sleeps at the barn and never fails to appear there at chore time for warm milk from his sardine can. He always chooses my little rocking chair by the heater to curl up on for a nap when he comes to the house in cold weather and the boys bring him in. No matter how sound asleep he appears to be, if anyone slightly rattles the lid on the bread box, he immediately comes over to "meow" for some bread, his favorite delicacy. In the summertime he stretches out on top of the wood box outside of the door and greets me with a gentle "mew" when I step forth; he follows me to the clothes line to roll at my feet for attention; he follows me to the garden, coming now and then to be petted. (One day he startled me so that I nearly keeled over when he playfully jumped at my hand from the other side of some potato plants I was weeding.) If I walk around the corner of the house toward the chicken house, he hurries to get ahead of me, then walks down the trail, holding high his waving tail, until we reach the hen house door where he gets "all set" to spring in after a mouse. Sometimes, when he wants to stay, I leave him with the chickens all night.

Another stray male cat came to the barn, but not to the welcome of Gray Tom—he didn't want a stranger drinking from his sardine can! Every day the boys "Haw haw hawed" at the hair-raising comedy of the two cats chasing each other around the barn, scaring the cows, rolling in the manure, fighting and biting and squalling and jumping at each other. After a few weeks, the stray cat went on his way and Gray Tom reigned supreme again, until a month ago when a black, long-haired, female cat moved in under the granary. She isn't especially friendly, but once in a while the boys can get close enough to pet her.

Now, she is the one who has the cute, little family; and I have warned the boys that they should dispose of most of them while they are small. But nothing doing! Every day each boy crawls up through the straw to see and admire them, and to put them back if they have tumbled from their nest.

June 30 Turning Bundles for Mice

All through the spring we had dry, cold weather. The drought and frost together stunted our alfalfa into only half its regular growth. By June 20 it was still freezing if the sky cleared at night; and when the drought was at last broken by rain, the rain refused to stop, setting us behind with our haying. Then after we did start haying, the rain poured again on our bales, soaking the ground to such an extent under them that we decided to turn them over to dry when the weather cleared again.

Dan and I spent most of one day walking up and down the fields on

The Eighty, turning the bales over. No one bothered to tell me, until we were through, that all of the bales should have been rolled onto their narrow edge, so that the field mice wouldn't crawl underneath and chew the baling twine in two!

July 2 *The Red Signal*

If there was anything wrong with that electric fence around the north hay field, I was determined to find it. The boys had decided the electric controller had gone "haywire" because they had fixed the fence wire just before haying had started, but already the red light blinked all of the time, indicating a short, and dozens of range cattle were slipping into the alfalfa field each day.

After the boys took off for the hay field, I saddled Prince, turned the current off the electric fence so that I couldn't get shocked while examining the line, and rode up to chase the cattle out of the alfalfa. Then, bending low from the saddle, I rode around the fence, removing all of the weeds and grass that had grown or been trampled against the wire. "That will surely do the trick," I said as I rode back to the barn. But when I turned on the controller, it still flashed red.

The next morning after the cattle were again driven from the field, I decided to tie the horse to a willow tree and walk completely around the fence where it went over the rocky hill and under the thorn thickets. On the hill I found a loose barbed wire in contact with the electric wire, and, under the bushes, an insulator turned toward a post. "Now I'm sure I've corrected the trouble," I boasted to myself. But again the light flashed red, and on the third morning the cattle were again chewing and trampling the alfalfa!

This time I knew that I would have to examine the end of the wire on the other side of the creek. I had put it off because I hadn't wanted to ford the deep water up at the end, nor ride back up from the barn side. But now, after running the cattle out again, I came back to the crossing and rode back up the creek. No wonder the fence wouldn't work—a cow had evidently run through the wire, tearing it entirely loose from the gate post. As well as fixing the wire back up, I had to remove big mullein weeds and thorn twigs that had grown over the fence during the rainy period.

Need I say—the red light flashed again! In the meantime, I suppose the cattle had knocked some more tall grass onto the wire. I never found out, because the next day the boys were ready to start moving equipment into the field, and the cattle were driven to the Lower Place.

July 3 *Ravin'?*

This summer, for some reason I don't remember and hope we never have again, we decided to raise some of the dairy calves instead of hauling them away to the sale yard. When haying started, I took over the night and morning job of mixing the dry, powdered calf feed in warm water and taking it to the four healthy-looking calves. The buckets we used were the ones with rubber nipples extending from the lower sides, so that the calves could suck slowly and naturally without having to stick their heads in at the tops of the buckets.

Before long, the smallest of the calves began to lose weight and wouldn't drink his milk. Before he died, another one grew sick. Before the second one died, a third one was sick. He died, too, leaving only the largest, which didn't appear to contract the disease.

"Never more!" quoth the ranchwife. "No more buying of all that expensive calf feed, and doing all of that work for the liability side. We could have bought veal calves cheaper."

August 8 Green Tomatoes

DO

Irrigate.
Pick blackberries.
Tie Prince in yard to eat out the jungle-high weeds.
Irrigate.
Rejoice—hay all stacked.
Examine waist-high tomato vines for any sign of ripening fruit.
Beware of wasps on the raspberries.
Irrigate.
Prepare for grain combining.
Freeze early cauliflower.
Admire reddish-headed sparrow's tiny nest in berry bushes.
Irrigate.
Cut cabbage to make kraut.
Can snap beans.
Be thankful that peas and summer squash are already in locker.
Remember—frost could come in three weeks.
Notice yellow warblers eating the newly matured wild lettuce seeds—
the seeds with the tiny, fuzzy umbrellas for floating in the wind.
Irrigate.

August 10 The Moon Sees Me

When city cousins came to visit, we set up an old bedstead out under the trees to help alleviate the bedroom shortage. We intended to fix it for one of the boys, but when I finished spreading the covers that evening, it looked so inviting that Clark and I decided it was for us.

Now that the guests have departed, we are still enjoying the "camping out" atmosphere and will be reluctant to move back in. Fortunately, there are no mosquitoes here this summer. The evenings are cool with no inside walls to hold the heat. How I love to see the moon and stars twinkling through the boughs, and to go to sleep listening to the rhythmic cricket chorus and soft rustling of the locust leaves. Bats dart around under the limbs, and high in the branches overhead a little owl sometimes stutters out a crooning hoot.

The only thing that bothers us is the Blue pup. He decided to keep us company by curling up on the ground at one side of the bed. Now and then he suddenly catches the scent of some kind of prowler, perhaps a skunk, and jumps up with a sharp "Yap." It does startle one out of the best of dreams!

August 12 Sauerkraut

I couldn't put off making sauerkraut any longer, although it is early in the season, because some of the cabbage heads were starting to split open. Before breakfast, while everything was crispy with dew, I gathered three dishpans full of cabbage from the garden and later informed the boys that they could do the cutting for me.

Then began the search for the kraut shredding board. I couldn't remember where I had hidden it away when I finished using it two years ago—not in the cellar—not in the little porch room—not in the kitchen cupboards—not in the garage—not in the woodshed; but, oh, yes, now I remember—up in the attic!

After I had trimmed off the outside cabbage leaves, the boys took turns at sliding the halved heads across the cutting blades in the board. As soon as they had cut a dishpanful, I dumped it into the big canner, sprinkled in a little salt, then stirred and punched it until the crisp, tender shreds were immersed in their own cool juice. Next, I packed it tightly in a three gallon earthenware crock and glass fruit jars.

This kraut making reminds me of the phonograph record we used to have when I was a kid—where Uncle Josh sang, "Sauerkraut is sunny . . . ho du li dil li . . . I stomp him and stomp him and make him nice and clean."

The most pressing problem (aside from cleaning bits of cabbage from the floor and everything else within reach) was where to set the containers for the fermenting process. The boys' Grandmother said, "Put it in the cellar immediately, as at this time of the year, the kitchen is too hot, and the kraut will sour too fast and spoil."

Husband warned, "The cellar is too cool and the kraut will all spoil instead of fermenting, if you put it there!"

Now who am I to decide such an issue? Ah, here is the answer—a compromise—I shall set part of it in each place and await the result. If both are right or wrong, and it doesn't spoil, when it reaches the right stage of sourness, I will process it in the jars in boiling water and set it away on the cellar shelves.

September 25 Lepto

One of our milk cows became sick and lost her calf a month before it was due. Then another did the same. Johnny's Berkshire sows suddenly lost their pigs.

In alarm, we called the veterinarian, as we feared brucellosis was in our herd. Tests were taken of all the milk cows, and we were surprised to learn from the results of the blood tests that, instead of brucellosis, our herd had another disease called leptospirosis. The cows will probably live through the epidemic, but Johnny's fall crop of pigs is lost, and there is a possibility of later abortions, also.

September 30 Harvest Mooning

Locust leaves are spotting with yellow. Bumper crop of wild thorn berries are falling to the ground. Elderberry bush is loaded down with powdery-blue berries, though I burned that bush to the ground last spring. Light frosts haven't harmed the hollyhocks blooming by the chicken pen.

This is fattening time of the year for the birds and animals that must prepare for the cold days ahead or the long trip south. The flocks of small song birds passing by here on their journeys from now until snow flies will be stopping for the oily weed seeds now bursting from their pods.

I fear it is also fattening time for me! When I go to the garden to get vegetables for the next meal, I can hardly refrain from gathering some of everything in sight. The fast-growing cauliflower heads are snowy white; the big, shiny-green, thick-meated peppers are crowding each other on the small plants; the yellow ears of corn are filled out just enough to be the sweetest and tenderest; the crisp, late cabbage heads are ready to burst; the carrots are golden and firm; the little refrigerator watermelons sound "thumping" ripe; a few red-ripe tomatoes peeking from the immense vines are belatedly trying to compete with the dainty, little, pear-shaped yellow tomatoes; slender, dark green cucumbers are just right to slice into vinegar with some of the tempting mild, white Bermuda onions; late string beans need gathering; slices of that zucchini summer squash would fry to a golden brown; a piece of baked and buttered pink, banana winter squash would be most delicious; late-ripening blackberries, looking like clusters of rich, ebony jewels, are coaxing to be popped into somebody's mouth before white frost arrives; tree-ripened prunes and peaches and pears, waiting to be canned, are sitting in baskets in the cellar.

Now I ask you, what are the odds against growing fat?

October 21 *Who Could Eat a Bear?*

This hunting season Johnny and Danny decided to take two saddle horses so that they could do their deer hunting over more territory on horseback.

I could hear them laughing as they forded the creek on their homeward way late in the afternoon. I watched them walking down the driveway, leading their horses, and wondered what kind of a funny, black saddle blanket the white horse was wearing. Soon I could see that it wasn't a saddle blanket at all. It was a black bear! And on Dan's horse was a deer!

What I could gather from the animated narration was that both animals had appeared on the side of the mountain at approximately the same time, causing the boys to have an exciting experience in downing both of them. This is surely putting it mildly; if the boys were to write the story, it would, no doubt, fill a whole chapter.

When I could get in a word, I asked them what they were laughing about down by the creek.

"We stopped at the creek to water the horses, and all those deer hunters in big, fancy cars coming down the road slowed up to take another look!" Again they laughed exultantly at how two little country chaps could show off their big game to the city fellows. I strongly suspected that they over-extended the horse watering period.

We had one problem with the bear. I suppose there are lots of people around here who eat bear meat, but we didn't know which ones and, having no telephone, we didn't have any easy way to locate them. We did find one neighbor who said she would *try* to find someone who would eat it!

The drouth we have had since June seems to be bringing the bears down from the timber to eat the thorn berries in the little ravines. The boys said there were more tracks of bear than of deer.

Even a pine squirrel has been chattering and chasing around in the trees by the house, much to the consternation of the dogs that are used to groundhogs or squirrels that run into holes or rock piles.

November 24 *Out for a Stroll*

Clark has been racing with the weather to get fall rye planted on The Eighty before a storm, reported by the weather bureau to be moving in from the Pacific coast, gets here. The boys will be home from school tomorrow, Thanksgiving Day, and will work in the field during the day, then we will have our dinner in the evening.

Having spent most of the day in the kitchen preparing food for tomorrow, I decided in the late afternoon to take a walk up the creek through the cow pasture for a bit of cool, fresh air. Wild mallard ducks swimming upstream from the barn rose into the air over the yellow-willowed banks, when they spied me on the trail above them. I examined the top of a beaver slide under a pile of old driftwood, and then noticed a little speckled owl sitting quietly on a thorn limb among the red leaves over my head.

Across the creek at the far end of the field, I saw and heard a tiny calf bawling as though hungry and lost. I yapped like a dog (if that were possible) to attract the mother cow. No cow appeared. I decided that the boys had better ride the horse across to investigate further at chore time.

Just as I was turning my steps back toward the house, I saw our guernsey milk cow lying quietly in a little slough. Before I ran down to see, I knew that she was dead. I thought perhaps she had been shot, as there was some blood on her neck, but I could find no bullet hole. Since the calf was evidently hers, perhaps she died of milk fever.

Anyway, the beautiful autumn day was spoiled for me and I wished that I had stayed at the house.

December 8 — Cat and Mouse Again!

Big discovery! Went to visit neighbors two or three miles away up over hills, started discussing cats, and learned that the black mother cat and kittens had moved up there! She had run away from their home in January and, becoming repentant or homesick, decided to return in November with her whole family. She had again hidden her smallest kittens, so we put two of the larger, black kittens in a box and returned them to our barn. Sometimes we see them jumping around on top of the baled-hay stack, which is almost a mouse paradise with its secret, little tunnels through good-chewing grain hay.

The boys call the larger cat "Sambo" because he is very quiet and dignified (or is it because he is so black?) waiting patiently for his warm milk. They call the other one just plain "Sam" because he meows constantly to be fed and comes up close to be "squirted" in the mouth with milk when they start washing the cows teats. Whether the two cats are enemies, or just rough, brotherly players, is a question, the way they slip up on each other from behind and bite and squeal.

December 25 — Christmas Day Menu

This is the first Christmas in several years that we have entertained at a family dinner with out-of-state guests. Most folks enjoy coming up into the hills to a "white Christmas." It is not easy to assemble ten or fifteen people in one room, but, believe me, it can be attempted.

There is plenty of space out of doors for the kids who bring along their sleds and skates and forget their overshoes.

For those future days when some of us may be poorer or richer, or alone, or forgetful and wonder what we had to eat in those "good old holidays," I shall leave this menu of today at our house:

1. Turkey — a twenty-pound, broad-breasted, which I stuffed and pushed into the oven at 5:45 a.m. in order to have tender by noon.
2. Stuffing — This recipe has been handed down from Clark's grandmother. It contains oysters; pre-baked, baking powder biscuits; onions; apples; celery; giblets and broth; dozen raw eggs; baking powder; salt; pepper; and sage.
3. Potatoes — mashed with cream.
4. Sweet potatoes — boiled and served plain with butter.
5. Corn — home canned, creamed.
6. Chicken pie — stewed hen covered with gravy and oven-browned biscuits.
7. Lime jello — containing apples and pineapple.
8. Celery — stuffed with cream cheese and sliced, ripe olives.
9. Shrimp salad — lettuce with broken shrimp and home-made dressing.
10. Dill pickles — from the cellar.
11. Pickled cauliflower — from the cellar.
12. Cranberry sauce — stewed at home.
13. Fruit jello — containing bananas, pineapple, orange juice, and topped with whipped cream and chopped black walnuts shelled at home.
14. Pies — blackberry, sour cherry, and apple.
15. Cake — applesauce fruit, baked two weeks previously.
16. Bread — white, homemade.
17. Butter — from creamery.
18. Raspberry jelly — from cellar.
19. Milk.
20. Buttermilk — from store.
21. Coffee — cream and sugar.
22. Candy — chocolates, home made fudge, brittles.
23. Nuts — mixed.
24. Popcorn balls — popcorn popped by Jimmy.

How I wish that my grandmothers, in the eighteen-hundreds, had written down their holiday menus and left them for me to read, cherish, and ponder over.

December 26 Picture Window?

Sitting at my typewriter this morning, the soft crackling of the pine fire in the heater at my back, I find that it is hard to keep my eyes and mind down on the paper and task at hand—they are continually being drawn out of the window before me.

This is, needless to say, no beautiful picture window decorated with frilly curtains or rich drapes or potted plants, but is, rather, two, small-paned windows sitting side by side with nothing to veil the view toward the south.

Two dry-grown locust trees, trunks tinted with yellowish-green moss, stand at the edge of the yard on a carpet of soft, unsoiled snow. From their rough, dark limbs hang clusters of brown seed pods and snow-frosted birds' nests. Round puffs of snow sit on hollyhock seed pods where bright pink and red petals once flared in tiers in the summer sun. This season's hues are more mellow—pale yellow dry grasses, russet syringa bushes.

Snow birds are flicking white, powdery bits from the brushy limbs of the thorn trees where they restlessly alight for a moment. Yearling, white-face calves drink fresh water from the tank on the other side of the snow-capped pole fence. Hopping and flying here and there, seeking possible scraps of food, are glistening, black and white, long-tailed magpies.

Beyond the trees, the rocky crags high up on the mountain stand out black above the speckled yellow, gray, and white of dry grass, buck brush, and snow. Not a trace of smoke, fog, or wind in the branches; yet over it all, swiftly floating, white, cumulus clouds, breaking more and more to let patches of deep blue sky show through.

— YEAR OF 1955 —

CLOSE TO SQUAW BUTTE

February 22 *Help Thy Neighbor*

This weather—always the weather! Persists in staying between zero and twelve above most nights. Already we have three calves frozen to death and brought two others to the house to revive.

A thoughtful neighbor stopped to tell us that one of our heifers up in the feedlot was having trouble dropping her calf. I thanked him kindly, but told him that Clark was away helping a neighbor, and I didn't think there was much that I could do about the heifer.

A few minutes later I decided that the two or three mile walk to get Clark wouldn't hurt me, so I buttoned up my winter wraps and started out.

When I reached the hills out of the protective canyon, how the freezing wind did blow! Climbing through the snow drifts made me puff, and when I gasped for more air, the whooping gusts of wind almost choked me. Being unfamiliar with the short-cut trails, I had to guess where they should be, which led me unsuspectingly into deep drifts.

How pleasant it was to take that last uphill step, knock on the door, and be admitted to a calm, warm kitchen!

After driving home, Clark found the heifer to be all right and the wee calf lying in a wind protected spot beside the feed bunks. We wondered about that. Later we learned that the neighbor had gone back to the feed yard to help the heifer himself, but couldn't catch her. So, several miles on down the road, he had stopped to tell my brother about the trouble. Brother drove up, aided the calf, returned home.

May 6 — Bath in the Hills

This spring we are venturing somewhat out of our old routine. We have rented a ranch almost adjoining ours but farther back in the hills and off the main highway—about two miles to the buildings. We decided to move for the summer as there will be green pasture for the hogs and milk cows, and a field sprinkling system to care for.

I am delighted to have a house, not only with a lovely new kitchen, but also with three bedrooms and a bath. A BATH! It has been so long since we have had a bathroom that it is a wonder we remember how to use it!

Clark needs to get the crops in and the fences repaired, but there is never a twenty-four hour period without rain, rain, rain, rain. So deep are the muddy ruts in the road that we have to use the tractor to get through or else walk through the fields.

May 16 — In the Mountains

A forsythia bush in bloom rises like a golden mist from the black soil and dark green leaves of the old apple orchard. A white cloud of plum blossoms lures the honey bees from their hive nearby. At one side of the lawn, just a jump down a steep bank, chuckles a little stream fed by cold springs. Sleepily sitting by the water are three white ducks, paying no attention to the threatening honks of the geese in the barnyard pond below.

West, behind the orchard, green mountains rise up to Squaw Butte. In all other directions, they lie down, over, beyond, behind, and up again.

The half-grown chicks are running around scratching for insects, picking grass and trying to find a way inside the yard fence. Pink peach blossoms peek through the kitchen window.

June 5 — Early Morn

When I awoke at 5:30 a.m., the sun was rising over the mountains and I could hear the trill of a meadowlark, the chatter of the bee martins, the crowing of a Chinese pheasant, the singing of the red and white hens wanting out of confinement, the honking of the pair of barnyard geese.

That reminded me—in the kitchen, tucked under a warm cloth in a grocery box, was that downy yellow and black gosling of theirs. Only they wouldn't claim him when I placed him gently by their sides, they knocked him for a roll. He is a cute little fellow, noisy just like his daddy, but that doesn't help.

When the goose didn't have any luck hatching her own, let her eggs get chilled or some stupid, unmotherlike thing, we put three of her fresh eggs under a setting chicken hen. She successfully hatched one, but she couldn't keep it because it didn't understand her language and kept wandering away.

Now I don't know what to do with him. One orphan gosling, no matter how cute, is a nuisance.

If those ornery, old, hissing birds would only take him!

June 15 — My Four Little Followers

When I step from the kitchen door there is always something for me to enjoy. First of all, the grass—it has been so long since we have had a lawn. It brings such a serene feeling to walk across the cool, neat, green grass, that I even delight in running the lawn mower! Next the flowers—I have to step aside just to bury my nose in one of the many, lovely roses; and step back to admire the white, exquisite balls that embellish the huge snowball bush; and always a velvety wonder to me are the soft, downy branches of the sumac trees. And the four little kittens—I can't resist reaching down to pick one up and cuddle it in my hand as they follow me to the garden gate.

I hadn't realized before that the personalities of cats are remarkably different. Here are four kittens all from the same litter of a long-haired, gray cat, yet none of them look like her.

Mitzi is the smallest—a shy creature with long, silky, black hair; delicate white feet, throat and nose. Her timid, low meow is hardly heard above the noise of the others. Every loud sound frightens her into hiding under the old cellar door.

Teddy Bear is always crying loudly for something to eat, as her rusty-black, long, shaggy hair carefully tries to dodge around my feet and into the house when I open the door. Climbing seems to be her specialty—while the others are running through the culvert and playing in the grass at my feet, she climbs the highest gate post and sits there waiting for a pat from me, or else she scrambles up the peach tree and slaps at the dangling, green peaches.

Purrless is similar in color to Mitzi, with coarser hair; but he never purrs, never meows, never expects to be petted. He isn't afraid; yet, when I do pick him up, he is as limp as a half-empty sack of beans.

Lazy Belle's short, tiger-striped fur is often curled up in a little, gray, round, sleeping ball. She has more dignity, likes to be petted occasionally, but not too much. She is braver, more adventuresome around the dogs. If she wants her head petted, she rears up on her hind feet, just like a horse. Especially, she likes to be carried, and climbs to my shoulder where her claws dig in tightly for a steady hold as we walk up through the old orchards.

While I am hanging clothes (over the precious lawn), I laugh to see the four soft, furry little fellows rolling and nipping at each other around my feet.

These aren't all of the cats on this ranch—at the dairy barn there is a gray mother cat with three kittens; a big, black, tom cat sleeps in the hay barn; and the before-mentioned, itinerant, long-haired, black, mother cat has four wild, black babies hiding along the little stream in the thickets.

July 15 Irriga-toiling

It was somewhat of a joke on me—thinking with all this roomy house that I could invite friends and relatives up for Sunday dinners. I hadn't anticipated a sprinkling system that would also sprinkle the dirt roads in certain spots at unpredictable times, making the dobey mud impassable for modern cars!

Every day is irrigating day—for me, either the garden or cow pasture by the chicken house, the lawn and flowers, the strawberries or raspberries, the hillside calf pasture, the garden above the house, or the garden and pasture down at the home place; for the boys, the hog and cow pastures, and the sprinkler irrigated hay fields. The boys, and even the hired man, complain about the difficult task of moving the sprinkler pipes night and morning, wading and staggering through the muddy ups and downs trying to balance the long, springy, cumbersome, teetering pipes.

The water is fed through these pipes by gravity from the spring water in the creek some distance above the house. It is my job, night and morning, to walk up there and remove all of the leaves, sticks, and bugs that have accumulated on the screen guard; and to chink up all of the surprising leaks that have appeared in the little dam.

This might be an irksome duty, if the dogs didn't follow companionably at my heels, and the kittens didn't scamper through the bushes trying to keep up. Then, too, it is pleasant walking through the old apple orchards, looking at the giant, gnarled trunks of the ancient grape vines, comparing the green fruit of the pears and plums, dipping hands into the falling water where frogs splash into the pool, and the air has that delicious, damp-foliage odor—all in the cool of the morning and evening.

Thus begins and ends the day.

August 19 Mighty Mites

One dark night we moved my white hens to their new summer home and set them in the hen house on roosts separate from the red hens. I supposed that the next night, after they had quit quarrelling with the red strangers, they would roost with them; but, no, they continued to roost by themselves, and even laid their eggs in different nests!

By the tough appearance of one old, speckled rooster and the way he flew at me with his claws, I suspected there might have been some fighting blood mixed with the New Hampshire red. I *really* believed it when I put two red hens under the same wooden lettuce crate to break them from setting, and one hen pecked the other to death! No wonder my gentle hens don't want to associate with such criminals.

There is one fussy, lone bantam hen with feathers on her legs that is so high strung she nearly flares into hysterics whenever I discover her hidden nest of eight eggs and destroy them. She doesn't understand that her eggs are rotten, and that I don't want her sitting out in the weeds, where a "varmint" might catch her at night.

Try as I do, I just can't keep the chickens out of the yard. I have woven boards and wire into every hole that I have found, pegged down the wire netting, and now I keep a pair of sheep shears handy to clip the wing feathers of all those I can catch that fly over the fence. Still, plenty get in.

One sunny morning I discovered a few mites crawling on my hands in the house where the young Austra-whites were roosting. In a few days the minute pests had multiplied until they were congregating in masses on hidden sides of the roosts. Then I found some of them in the coop with the mother hen and her little ones; next, in the house with the old hens.

Action had to be taken before those bloodsucking villains killed all of my fowls. Having read in a farm magazine that malathion dust, sprinkled around on the roosts and floor, was the best, new remedy, I drove to town to purchase some of the insecticide. But when I got there the cupboard was bare. The feed store had burned the night before! No other store that we could think of near by stocked malathion, so the proprietor managed to find a can of pentachlorophenol and told me to mix it with oil and spread it around on the roosts. Now I had had earlier experience with using black crankcase oil in chicken houses, and I didn't enjoy the thought; but I thanked him just the same and returned home, knowing what a distasteful job I had ahead of me.

If I had had a big spray gun, it wouldn't have been quite so bad, but I had to make a dauber out of a stick and a rag and smear the penta-oil mixture everywhere inside the houses where mites gather in the daytime. At first, about the only effect I could see was that I had oily blouses, jeans, and shoes; a lasting, nauseous scent; and a nose bleed after each session of daubing. But gradually the mites have disappeared until the few that are left may do no more harm.

I have had chicken troubles before in my life, and hope this will be the last.

September 4 Ululation

In the pre-dawn we are often wakened by the sudden staccato yelps of coyotes back in the hills. Immediately the dogs try to prove that they can howl just as loud and just as long as any old coyote.

Several times at dusk we have seen a large animal outside of the yard fence, but always it has run away before we could distinguish what it was. One night some kind of an animal dragged one of my chicken fryers from under the chicken house door and ate it right on the steps. How any "varmint" could get its big paw in, let alone pull a half-grown chicken through such a small crack, I will never understand. However, the evidence—blood and feathers and all—was there. It must have been a bobcat with such long, strong claws that it mashed the chicken before pulling it out.

A few of the red hens hide their nests out around the barnyard and hatch some chicks to hunt their own living. Every time that I think the fryers will soon be large enough for the pan, they disappear.

October 11 Tons? Are You Sure?

I declare, from the bucketfuls of apples that I have gathered off the lawn and dumped over the fence, that old tree *must* have produced sixteen tons this year! A fruitman friend of ours says it is the largest apple tree that he has ever seen in any orchard or any other place. The apples weren't too delicious when cooked; but, raw, they were good for my health, as there were always fresh, shiny-red falls tempting me as I crossed the grass to the clothesline or visited the garden—no poison spray to worry about. Most of the small apples from the gnarled old trees up and down the creek and in the orchards fell to the ground for hog feed.

I got the most fun out of harvesting wild plums—little, pinkish-yellow fruits, no larger than the end of my little finger, hidden in the thickets up the hill along the little creeks. I have probably canned enough wild plum preserves to last us the rest of our lives!

October 20 What Is That Crawling in My Bed? Ouch!

When I go upstairs in the mornings to make the beds, I take along a broom and dust pan to sweep up the piles of wasps that the boys have slaughtered the night before. Where so many get in or come from, I don't know. All old buildings and especially school houses here are infested with them, yet the likes of this one, I have never before seen. On sunny, warm afternoons they sail around the roof thicker than honey bees around a hive.

November 25 The Big Freeze

We have had a terrible freeze—untimely for the middle of November. The unseasonable warm weather during the fall kept the trees, and shrubs, and vines from going into their dormant state. This let the freeze catch them with their green leaves on, which may be a death blow.

It is an eerie sensation to hear the frozen, brown leaves flapping on the tree limbs and to see them falling on top of the snow—snow that should have fallen on top of the leaves.

December 2 Pork Poor

We have moved back to our own ranch where the boys can more easily reach the school bus, and the distance isn't so far to haul the milk to the road.

All of our work of raising pigs from fifteen sows went for nothing. So poor was the selling price that we didn't get nearly as much money for them as we had put into feed grain. Some of the weaner pigs sold as low as two dollars apiece. It was far cheaper this year to buy pork than to raise it.

December 27 Flood

Just before Christmas the warm wind and rain decided suddenly to get rid of all the snow. Water dashed down every ravine to join the roily waters of the big Squaw Creek.

I gave the alarm after I walked up to get the mail and looked back down on the gray water creeping over the foot of the garden.

Our irrigation pump sits on a platform several feet out into the creek. We are always a little concerned when ice and high water come along. This time the water completely covered the platform. Clark hurried to the shop for wrenches to undo the rusty bolts holding the pump to the platform planks, while Johnny rushed for the tractor and trailer and backed them in as close as possible through the water. It was a clumsy place to work on the narrow, water-hidden, slick boards; even so, they managed to lift the heavy pieces into the trailer and pull them to safety without falling into the icy water.

Farther up the creek only the tops of the fence posts were visible above the water. An old hay wagon bobbed up and down, held by a barbed wire fence.

— YEAR OF 1956 —
LISTEN!

February 1 *Hoo Hoo*

The great horned owl's soft hooting, carrying through the black of night across the wild thickets and ravines, has always been a pleasure to me. In my mind I can see him sitting almost straight up atop the largest branch, slowly turning his tufted head from side to side on his bronze body, his round, black eyes closing now and then as he relaxes his vigil to send forth his call.

However, when two of those night predators alight on top of the house in the dead of night and start arguing, it is much different. Their soft hoots have turned blatant, and they prolong each one with a raspy, choking screech, allowing no lull in between their frictional outcries.

Last night perhaps they were arguing over a mangled rabbit held prey in their vicious talons. Anyway, I was about to leave the warm comfort of my bed to throw something at them, when the dogs decided it was also too much for them, and in competition, or retaliation, they began a howling uproar around the house. Soon all was quiet—the noise had vanished with the silent swish of great horned owl wings.

March 4 *Rock Hound*

Everything out of doors was heaped and hung with heavy snow—even the sides of the fence posts were plastered. As soon as the waffle bowls were washed and the favorite Sunday radio sermons were over, I put on my wraps and started out for a few minutes of outdoor enjoyment. As I slowly ascended the mountain, the clouds were moving swiftly, forming a dark, menacing fog over the deep blue timber line to the north, and, to the south, a break of light blue sky where sun shone over snowy hills.

Not a speck of soot or smoke marred the cleanliness of the new snow and air. Not an odor from any plant; the dusty-green leaves of the sage had sealed in their redolence from the cold weather. Not a track of any wild animal was in sight. The storm of the night had kept wild life confined to their dens and thickets. Two wild geese flew up the creek, honking their familiar way on a short-cut pass over a ridge.

I followed an old road, plashy with deep horse tracks and partly overgrown with sagebrush. The sound of water trickling down over rocks led me up a small notch, where I stood at the foot of a large, outcropping rock, watching the cold snow water spilling down the steep crevices to drench soft tufts of green moss. I climbed up around the side of the massive rock to look at the cascading stream from above. The babbling of this tiny stream near me had drowned out the constant roar of the roily creek water far below. Startled partridges, finding protection here under the bushes from the cold wind on the ridges, flew higher up the ravine.

I stooped to pick a queer, molten-appearing rock from the water. Then I noticed several whitish stones of bird egg size embedded in the bedrock, and wished that I had carried Dan's rock-pick hammer with me. Like an old prospector, hot on the trail of precious metals, I clambered upstream, using the big stepping stones for a stairway, while searching for more stones. My coat pocket began to fill with little, round, yellow, bead-like stones resembling petrified seed pods, with only part of the hard outer shell left. I didn't know how to identify the names of rocks or minerals, but I would put them with Dan's collection of rocks and fossils in the old ice box sitting behind the woodshed.

A far off rifle shot reminded me that it was time to prepare Sunday dinner, that I was quite high on the mountain, and that my gloves were wet. The sun was now shining warmly, and sagebrush limbs were flipping into the air wherever a load of snow fell from them.

The descent proved to be more slow and difficult than the ascent; however, I didn't slip or sit in the water (no, not much!). On the way down, I decided that when our boys are grown and gone from home, if obsolescence threatens, and if I need additional activities (can you imagine such a thing on a ranch?), I will join a mineral club and learn to hunt thundereggs.

Guess what? When I walked in the door, fried chicken was sizzling in the pans! How nice to have a husband who knows how to cook.

July 3 Phantasmagoria!

We don't live close enough to any side roads to hear vehicles other than those that travel on the asphalt road not far from our house. Even so, several times lately I have wakened at dawn to hear a truck approaching. I hear it shifting up and down, up and down, up and down the hill. Its pulling motor suggests power and a big load. Then the sound of the motor dies away—then comes back, yet never arrives or passes by! This phantom truck is haunting me, since I have been unable to come to any sound conclusion as to its reality.

Another weird sound, which I *can* explain, comes from an old broken-down tractor that sits beside the path to the barn. As I walk by it, I am sometimes startled by a low, eerie murmur vibrating from its innards. It gives an uncanny feeling that the ghost of the old wreck is trying to bring it back to life. Actually, I found the sound to be the muffled buzzing of bumble bees, emerging from a nest deep within a round, steel pipe.

Out in the old milk house, some baling wire had been thrown down in a pile with gunny sacks and pieces of baling twine. Whenever I went to switch off the electric fence controller, one certain wire sticking up in the way always annoyed me; but when I gave it a pull to dislodge it, immediately an angry volume of buzzes arose. I didn't stay longer to see if the angry bumble bees came out! Now, whenever I go in there, I give the wire a gentle touch, just to see, and always the slight tremor instantly alerts them.

July 21 Mountain Bluebird

"Oh, isn't that a cute little nest?" I exclaimed to a cousin who was helping to pick blackberries early one morning.

Smaller than a teacup, lined with down, securely fastened to the thorny berry canes, completely hidden from overhead eyes, it tenderly held four of the tiniest blue eggs. On top of the four lay another egg twice as large and whitish colored with black scratches—the deposit of an English sparrow, too lazy to hatch its own. As no mother bird was in sight, I removed the larger egg, taking care not to touch the nest.

Next berry-picking day, when I peeked into the hidden nest, there were four, little, open mouths pointing up from bare skins and tiny tufts of down. The sound of rustling leaves had caused them to instinctively open their mouths for the insect they expected Mama Bird to bring for breakfast. I glanced around inquiringly, for where was the mother of these infants? There on the fence near me, twitting excitedly, was a feathered piece of turquoise—a mountain bluebird. Sometimes I had heard the sweet warbles of bluebirds in the creek thickets, but because of their shy, wild natures, had never had a chance to observe them closely.

On the next trip to the berries, I was surprised to see that the tiny ones had grown so large that they completely filled the little nest. Still, they were not mature, and I wondered what would happen to them when there wasn't household room to hold all.

I never found out, for, when berry-picking day came again, only a few dry grasses remained. The nest had disappeared, been torn down by a marauder. I suppose, when the little ones began to chirp and wriggle above the edges of the nest, a cat or other animal discovered their presence and claimed them for his supper; or maybe they had grown large enough to flutter out of reach.

July 31 Hay Elevator

Every year on this ranch some new machinery or equipment is needed and has to be purchased; either an old piece wears out or is outmoded (such as horse drawn equipment). If these things didn't wear out, deteriorate, and depreciate so fast, and if there was enough land to keep them busy, it might be profitable to buy them. This is one of the reasons back of the trend toward larger acreage—to try to keep the necessary machinery working enough weeks in the year to make it pay its way.

This year we bought a hay elevator, which is quite a labor-saving machine, and almost a "must" for stacking baled hay. One person places the bales, one at a time, in the chute at the bottom of the lift, where an endless chain pulls them to the top and drops them off onto the high stack.

In these times when it is almost impossible to hire men for harvest jobs, work they formerly did has to be replaced as much as possible with the help of high-priced machinery.

August 4 Bragging Bulls

Shortly after we had gone to bed in the tent (set up to serve as an extra bedroom when guests were here), an awful screeching noise sounded from the cow pasture. Now, any person familiar with livestock and wire fences recognizes the terrible sound of barbed wire being stretched and wrenched away from posts and stables by the powerful pull of a large animal. Usually, after several kicks and lunges, the wire will break or loosen and the animal comes free.

But this time the tweaking and rasping continued on and on. I didn't want to waken Clark, as he was working sixteen hours a day (including traveling time) in the woods. Knowing from the mad bellows that a bull was involved, I quickly discarded the notion of my going to investigate! Nearly all livestock will grow panicky when held fast by a wire, and jerk and struggle until the barbed wire has cut long gashes in their flesh. Obviously, the bull couldn't be left in the entanglement until morning; reluctantly, I got up and, hoping they were braver than I, called Jim and Dan to investigate.

Armed with flashlights and wire-cutting pliers, they advanced across the pasture in the direction I pointed out. The screeching had stopped, and all that they could find was a hole in the fence where the bull had gone through.

What a relief this was to me—now I could relax and sleep—or could I? The quiet was quickly shattered. Evidently, from the clamor arising on the night air, the bull had entered the pasture to have a duel with the one already in. First one would let loose with an ear-splitting "Mawooo, mawooo, mawooo"; then the other would respond with mad snorts and roars of "Baaaw, baaaw, baaaw." As though that weren't ferocious enough, a third bull in the barnyard joined in with belligerent "Grrrr's" equal in volume to at least one-hundred dog power!

The sound of their fierce and brutal natures carried especially loud into the tent where I lay shivering and perspiring, expecting at any moment to hear their long, sharp horns clashing in combat. I wondered if the fighting bulls in Mexico made such unearthly bellows, and how anyone could be brave enough to face them. I also wondered if the milk cows were lying peacefully chewing their cuds, or were they standing around wide-eyed waiting for the fight?

The bulls must have bluffed each other out, as the noise died down; however, not to let each other forget, they resumed their uproar again at midnight. I don't care if I ever hear another bull bellow!

October 15 Gone Huntin'

At this time of the year, when the bloom is on the sage, there is no doubt but that this is a predominantly masculine household. Rifles and shotguns and scabbards standing in corners, red felt hats and red shirts thrown on the floor, ammunition rolling from tables and shelves, ramrods and whetstones and hunting licenses and deer tags getting misplaced, gun and boot oil perfuming the air, dangerous hunting knives emerging from forgotten places in drawers; match holders and lighters being refilled, and this sort of conversation going on:

> "Shall we walk up Four Mile or drive around the old road?" "Shall we take Prince in the truck or go in the old black ford?" "Wonder if Bob will get here in time to go with us?" "We could hear shooting all around us!" ". . . . lots of fresh tracks, but didn't see one deer." "I missed her the first time but when she jumped I fired again." "I think I aimed too high down that hill." "Where is my old denim lunch sack?"

and so forth and so forth.

This isn't all of the indications, either. When hunting luck hits and game starts pouring in, there are ropes and single-trees and pulleys and skins hanging in the trees by the house; feathers and feet and heads and bones being dragged all over the yard by the dogs; blood and wild-scent saturated clothing to stuff into the washing machine; late suppers; many hours involved in cleaning, cutting, sawing, grinding, and wrapping meat for the freezer.

Whoever saw such lucky hunters! This was Jim's first try at big game hunting—he hadn't even fired the rifle before. The boys were sitting on a log in the timber eating their lunches when Jim glanced across a clearing, and there stood a group of elk! In amazement he said, "Look over there," then jumped up, grabbed his rifle, aimed, and shot a big cow elk. At that same instant the other elk leaped and plunged down over the mountain toward safety; but Dan, in fast pursuit, managed to take aim at a big calf and downed it before it could reach the cover of the underbrush and pines.

At 1:30 p.m. Jim drove in and said, "Mother, you'll have to go with me. We've killed two elk and I'll have to take Prince up in the truck to pack them out to the road. Dan and Bob stayed up there to clean them out and I can't haul Prince all of the way in because the road is too steep and rough."

Quickly I hung the last of the washing on the line, set my kettle of bread dough in the refrigerator, and left a note for Clark—"Gone huntin'. Please punch down dough in refrigerator!"

It was quite a long drive up into the mountains to the hunting grounds. When we reached the beginning of the steepest part of the road, and unloaded Prince on a handy cut bank, I happened to remember that we were in dangerous territory and that in my haste, I had completely forgotten to wear any red clothing! Someone might mistake Prince for an elk. Jim solved the problem by loaning me his red felt hat before I mounted to ride several miles through strange timber on an old wood road.

Luck was with us, as Jim drove nearly all of the way in; and other young hunters who came along kindly helped to load the heavy elk quarters onto the horse. After they made three pack trips to the truck with the horse, I was again in the saddle, hurrying out over the difficult trail road. The old truck nosed slowly through the soft, rutty tracks, bumping over boulders and around sharp turns. The late afternoon was turning into dusk; if Jim failed to swerve enough to miss a big rock, or if he settled into a soft hole so that the truck couldn't pull out, we would have a cold, rough night ahead of us.

Thank goodness, none of those foreboding things happened. The truck held together, no one shot us, the horse was loaded again, and it was 8:00 p.m. and very dark when we drove into the ranch.

For me there was supper to cook; for the boys, meat to clean and hang to cool. Clark had done the chores, and made arrangements for me to accompany him on a 250 mile trip the next day starting at 5:00 a.m.

After supper I wearily stacked the dishes at the sink, jammed the bread dough back into the refrigerator, and dropped into bed.

October 30 Cacophony

One of our black gilts that farrowed down by the creek didn't want to take her litter of pigs to the barn to sleep; she did compromise by moving them half way. The halfway mark was the baler shed, just a few feet from the yard fence and not far from the open window at the head of our bed.

I didn't know before that pigs grunted and grumbled at each other so much during the night. Grunting alone wouldn't have been so bad if they hadn't let loose with those piercing, hair-raising shrieks that, so far as I know, only a hog can make. At near intervals all night came those harsh squeals, then a big hubbub of loud, shrill wails as, evidently, they took quick turns at biting each other.

I tried everything I could think of to discourage them from their sleeping quarters. I drove them to the barn after dusk, but they slipped around through the rocks and sagebrush, and beat me back! I put rocks and posts in their nest. When that had no effect, I tried rolls of barbed wire. Now this last did discourage them, so they rooted another nest out in the open a few feet closer to the house!

I lay awake at nights (how could I do anything else?) trying to think of some way to get rid of them, short of shooting. But I never thought of the right thing until after the first autumn rain wet down their nest and sent them to the barn to sleep. If only I had turned the hose of cold water over them!

November 28 Left Over? Freeze It Up!

Stuffed full to the edge, that's our home freezer. Twenty-five cubic feet in an upright freezer is a lot of space to fill, and for a while (over a year, in fact, since we bought it), I began to think we never would get it completely full. Wild game did the trick—two elk and three deer make a lot of wrapped meat.

I find that people have as much difference of opinion on which foods freeze well as they do on "which is the best doctor." One friend tells me that her family won't eat frozen bread because it tastes saltless. I bake six large loaves at once and freeze all in excess of what we can eat while it is fresh, so that I won't have to bother to bake as often.

Another family thinks that corn on the cob is the best luxury of a freezer—our family won't touch it! A relative bakes an oven full of potatoes, freezes them in aluminum foil, and finds them quick and wonderful to warm up. Others who tried this method decided that it took so long and so much oven heat to warm them that they might as well bake fresh ones. The first potatoes I tried to serve in this way had frozen spots in the center—for an unexpected guest!

I receive all kinds of recipes for freezing sandwiches and waffles and cakes and pies. If I need to prepare in advance for emergencies or extra busy days, it is a big help; otherwise, my family says, "Never serve frozen foods if they can be prepared fresh, because they are only second best."

Electricity with its refrigerators and freezers has greatly changed the eating habits and menus of rural people. It used to be that we could have fresh red meat only in the cold, wintry days when it wouldn't spoil. Meat for summer use had to be safely canned in jars or heavily smoked and salted. That was why so much chicken was served on Sundays—the only fresh meat quickly available.

December 1 First Aid First

At last an opportunity came to enroll in a Red Cross first aid class. Yes, an opportunity, even though we had to drive almost fifty miles two nights a week in order to attend.

We learned many things that we should have known long ago. I am glad to have this Standard Certificate, but still realize that it is far less than what we need. Too much material must be studied in too few hours. I wonder how long this quickly scanned knowledge will stay with me.

More than ever, I still feel that first aid, along with atomic survival, should be taught from the first grade through the eighth. Perhaps it would then stay with a person for life, and be easy to splint an arm at the scene of an accident as to pull on shoes and socks in the mornings.

December 29 Kitchen Designing

Looking at pretty pictures of, and reading about, convenient kitchens is certainly different from designing one. I found that in order to have one convenience, I had to sacrifice another. For instance, if I had big windows for light, I had to give up several wall cupboards; if I left plenty of space over the counters, the upper shelves were too high for me to reach; if the counters all ran on an even level with the sink, they were too high for mixing; if I placed the refrigerator, sink, and range conveniently close together, there would not be enough near work counters, but there would be too much heat on the refrigerator, or grease and water splattering; if I filled in all of the area under the counters with shelves or drawers, there would be no comfortable place to sit at work on a high stool; and so it went.

"You will have to draw the plans for your cupboards," Clark warned me, although I didn't realize at the time that it was a warning. It was a simple sounding assignment. For plans and materials and color combinations, I looked in numerous magazines. The home demonstration agent gave me pamphlets. Home decorators in the stores were very considerate of my needs. The yardstick for measuring all imagined angles was indispensable. Pencils and papers were kept handy for quickly thought-up arrangement diagrams.

No matter how respectable the plans looked on paper, they never measured out right. I finally eliminated all fancy, turning, corner shelves; drop-down bins; drawers on rollers; partitioned shelves; etc. They were too hard to make, too expensive, or (more likely), too hard to draw plans for!

As we had to put a new roof over our cellar, we decided to build a room on the cement foundation and put the roof over that. If we succeed in getting a kitchen-living room built here, perhaps some day we may be able to add a few more rooms to it.

— YEAR OF 1957 —
AT LAST

February 2 Farm Sales

Each year in our community there are one or two farm sales. Country people are sorry to lose long-known neighbors and friends from their valley. The sale usually means that there has been a death in the family, or the owner has lost his health, or is getting too old for the hard work, or he cannot make a living and also meet his obligations. However it isn't always sad; once in a great while, owners are selling because they are looking forward to a better farm or position or living conditions.

Getting ready for the sale is a big job for the owners. The machinery must all be pulled to convenient spots where auctioneers and people can gather around to look. All new and old tools and forgotten pieces of this and that must be carried forth and placed on wagons or platforms where they can be inspected by prospective buyers and exhibited by the auctioneers. Furniture for sale is moved out into the yard, weather permitting, so that people can pull the drawers and sit on the springs and find all the defects. Livestock must be kept in stalls or pens and each listed by name and production record.

Ranch men never miss these sales if they can help it. There is lots of good-natured banter over prices paid, or useless items bidded in, and maybe a chance to purchase a good milk cow, or a needed implement, or a priceless item hidden at the bottom of a box of junk. For those who came long distances before noon to inspect the goods, and for those who grow hungry or want to visit over a cup of coffee, a refreshment stand is set up near the house by women of community clubs or church organizations. They are kept busy serving hamburger or chicken sandwiches, potato salad, homemade pie, coffee, and lemonade.

The lady of the farm house hurries from one place to another with a forced smile on her nervous face as she answers innumerable questions, for she is saying goodbye to precious things that have meant so much to her for so many years. Her house is often thrown open for the convenience to buyers and for rest rooms for the visiting women. She hears her dear old furniture belittled, and sold for a fraction of its value. Flowers and shrubbery that she has spent so many hours perfecting are trampled to the ground. She hurries away to hide her tears when the old, pet cow that has been so gentle and faithful is led away to a strange trailer.

We see laughter and tears mingled at an institution that is perhaps as old as the tilling of land itself, and will, no doubt, continue into the future as long as men own farms.

May 30 What! No Calendars?

If my daybook lacked entries for several months, I will say it was mostly because my extra time was spent in working on the new kitchen-living room. It seems that we are always getting ourselves involved in more work than we envision before it starts.

I won't mention all the measuring, sawing, sanding, glueing, perfataping, hole filling, undercoating, fitting, bonding, figuring, painting, searching for materials, wiring, shortage in orders, etcetera.

This do-it-yourself work is rewarding to creative souls, but they need to have had experience beforehand. After all the mistakes we made, I believe that I could write a long article of advice to the beginners. Directions on the materials always tell you what to do but not what not to do—like dribbling contact bond down on drawers that later have to be painted!

Most everyone admires the peninsula with its double sink, primrose yellow hard top, and stainless steel edging; but not a person has complimented me on the open spice shelf that I like so much. There was some thought of leaving the exterior of the cupboards in natural varnish; however, I decided that if painted white they would reflect more light and more nearly match the white refrigerator and electric range, yellow work tops, and three tones of bluish green on walls and ceiling. For (hoped for) relaxing, we have at one end of the room a brown daveno and chair to blend with the brown and buff speckles in the sand-colored, vinyl floor tiling. Lying on the lamp table that Clark made from the same materials used in the kitchen counters is the Bible, with Jim's sagebrush lamp and Dan's pine book ends. In the center of the room sits the old, round, oak table (legs painted black to match the kitchen toeholds) for a "gathering around" place to eat, talk, and sort mail.

Here is an example of the thought that must go into every small selection that a person makes. After spending hours looking at curtains, shades, and materials, I finally decided on plain, white, match stick bamboo cafes for the following reasons: I could buy them in different lengths to fit my odd sized windows; they fold compactly against the walls, out of the way of furniture and stove hazards (ruffly, fluffy, or starched materials do not); when drawn, they may serve as sun shades; if I later redecorate the walls, I can paint the curtains to match; work would be saved in sewing, as well as in washing and ironing; and they were inexpensive.

Pictures, the bigger the better, are one of my weaknesses. As I didn't have a majestic painting to hang on the one unbroken wall, I had to settle for nine smaller pictures here and there. Since there isn't room for that many at once without clutter, I have stored a few in the cupboard to rotate for a change of scenery. A person can't please everyone, or even all the members of one family, with a choice of pictures; so, if I rotate the "Old Mill Stream" with "Christ on the Mount of Olives," the "Dutch Windmill" with "Adam Naming the Creatures" (a Currier and Ives heirloom), "Olympia Park" with "Oahu Island," "Boulder Peak" with "Navajo Village," and keep the graduation pictures of the boys up continually (not to suit them), I may manage to please part of the family part of the time!

The Methodist Ladies graciously furnished flower planters to hang on either side of the south window over the peninsula. The gift philodendron plants in them are the first house plants that I have had in twenty years.

July 20 Seven Hundred

When we arrived at the back side of the Eighty to start loading bales, Clark said, "What do you suppose cut these strings? Looks like somebody poured acid on them." Some of the loops of twine were cut into three or four pieces, letting the packed hay fall loose at the ends. Almost every bale was cut on at least one of the two twine wraps.

"It can't be anything but grasshoppers chewing them in two," I decided. "Just look at those big, fat hoppers jumping and crawling all over the bales."

"But this twine was supposed to be chemically treated to resist insects and rodents," Clark protested ruefully. "Must be mighty poor hay, if they prefer eating the string."

There was nothing to do but return with balls of twine and start retying the bales by hand. Abandoning the driving job, I started plodding up and down the fields with twine and pocket knife. My jersey gloves were brought into use, because pulling the rough twine tautly around the bales soon brought blisters to my fingers. The men had leather gloves, but any kind of gloves are bunglesome when it comes to tying knots in string. Cotton gloves are terrible to wear when handling hay which is full of cheatgrass seeds—soon they look akin to porcupines, and the sharp points of the seeds start digging into the fingers. Very soon I gave up the impossible and time consuming chore of removing the stickers, until it was time to leave the field and to stuff the gloves into my pocket.

As sure as we found a bale lying flat-side down, so that the hoppers hadn't bothered it, either mice or gophers or ground squirrels had burrowed underneath and chewed the strings in two!

Clark decided this was too much of a waste of his time, and found another logging job. Jimmy hired a neighbor boy to help us. I started timing myself and found that (not counting the walking, and knife and twine picking up and putting down time) I could re-tie both strings on a bale in two minutes—what a wonderful accomplishment!

August 7 Drives You Buggy!

The variety of insects down in the garden. . . . I am beginning to wonder and feel apprehension. . . . How in the world did they all find their way to my garden away out here in these remote hills? It wouldn't be so bad to have to cope with two or three kinds of noxious bugs, or two or three kinds of poisons, but when they come by the dozen. . . . It seems that the more insecticides man perfects, the more he needs.

Just to illustrate, here is list of pests that try to destroy my garden:

1. blister beetles
2. cutworms
3. grasshoppers
4. black crickets
5. ants
6. asparagus beetles
7. black aphids
8. corn earworms
9. European earwigs
10. thrips
11. cabbage worms
12. onion maggots
13. strawberry worms
14. green aphids
15. wasps
16. beet leafhoppers
17. blow flies
18. yellow jackets
19. potato beetles
20. wire worms
21. tomato horn worms
22. black leaf hoppers

(This is in addition to a dozen or more kinds that bother around the livestock and buildings, and many others that I cannot identify.)

August 19 Please, No Thunder

The peculiar, sweet odor of sagebrush smoke may bring nostalgic memories to some people who had had picnic dinners or wiener roasts over sagebrush bonfires, but it brings alarm to dry-hill ranchers. At the first wisp carried on the breeze, they look out in all directions to try to locate the source of fire.

We have to drive up out of the canyon to look around, and usually find that the smoke and perhaps small cinders have drifted in over the mountains from many miles away. One summer evening, however, we did find a fire about three miles down the road in a steep, rocky canyon. As darkness came on, the roaring blazes cast great, flickering beams and shadows on the huge rocks of the rough canyon walls. It was terrifying to have the men lost from view in the deep shadows where we could hear them calling to each other. With the help of a bulldozer to plow out fire guard trails on the accessible side, they managed to control the fire between three creeks and the highway.

When our field machinery is not in use, we try to park it in sandy, bare, or green spots. The thick, deep growth of grass on the hills has caused a greater fire hazard than usual this season. In late summer the wild cheatgrass has grown yellow and dry—a more perfect form of tinder could hardly be found. The least little spark would leap into flames and bound over the ground and through the grass like flashes of lightning. Spreading fire might not only damage our homes and livestock, but most certainly would destroy the fall grazing for the cattle.

We shiver when we hear the grumble of thunder. Lightning nearly always strikes in a few places on the hills during a close electric storm. If rain falls, we are very thankful.

September 4 *Watch It or Else!*

A person should be extremely thankful for a good irrigation pump and plenty of water to run out onto the green pasture and garden. I'll have to admit, though, that at times I wish for the old spring where I turned the trickling water into the ditches and it ran down the hill through the garden without having to be watched all of the time. Especially do I wish when I get the pump primed, turn on the motor, and nothing happens—a fuse burned out! Or when the water suddenly stops coming and I run up through the pasture, climb the fence, and find the pump sucking air instead of water (which means that the water in the creek has dropped lower and that I will have to flatten an old wooden door down on the water and wire it into place so that air can't funnel into the pipe). Or when I have to remove my shoes and socks, roll up my jeans, and wade out into the cold water to remove, with my fingers, stringy moss from the foot of the pipe. Sometimes a snake has met his death against the force of the pulling water. Great gobs of snake and moss!

The irrigating water must also be kept under surveillance or it is apt to overflow where water weeds have unexpectedly grown, filling the ditch; or run through gopher holes back into the creek; or break the ditch bank where pigs dam with a dip; or wash through a headgate and flood out of bounds; or stagnate in pools and detour around the high, dry spots.

A friend of mine asks, "What have you been doing lately?"

I can't think of a thing but, "Oh, just irrigating."

September 11 — Tired?

Blue car	5
Old black car	5
Truck	7
Big trailer for hauling hay	4
Trailer for hauling baler across creek	2
Trailer for hauling stock	2
Dump trailer	2
Trailer for cattle feeding	2
Hay elevator	2
Tractor	4
Old tractor	4
Hay baler	2
Manure spreader	2
Grain drill	2
Hay rake	2
Hay mower	1
	48

Can you guess what all of these items have in common? If not, I'll tell you—inflated rubber tires. In maintenance of farm equipment, the last thing a person might think of is rubber tires, yet it may be one of the most expensive items in both time and money. Consider the task alone of keeping up 48 tires, plus a few spares, during the seasons of field work.

Thank goodness, my little garden tractor has solid rubber tires.

October 14 — Potato Digging Time

Clark wields the shovel, I pick the potatoes up out of the dirt and toss them into buckets, Jim carries them to the cellar.

We are always glad when the toil of potato digging day is over, and we can admire the potatoes stacked in their bin.

We have never had to buy a potato to eat since the first winter we were here on the ranch, and we have had a surplus for relatives, friends, and the preacher. One late winter when there were no potatoes on the market, we were glad to share ours with some of the neighbors. Good Idaho potatoes!

October 20 Gus Is Coming

"Gus is coming! Gus is coming!" my voice sang out to surprise everyone.

Later, Clark found the list in the cupboard—wash all the windows, haul off the trash, wax the floors, clean the cellar, cut down the weeds, prepare the bedding. . . . "What is all this for?" he asked in amazement.

"Why, don't you know? Gus is coming!"

"Mother, why are you carrying so many weeds?" Jim asked.

"Because Gus is coming!"

Later, "Mother, why are you baking so many rolls and cookies? Is the President coming?"

"No, but Gus is coming!"

My family shook their heads in bewilderment—maybe Gus was coming, but why was that so important?

I worked at the cleaning tasks with my hands, but my mind wandered back over the years to the winter of 1927 when Gus and I first became friends. In a little home magazine published in the South, she had found my printed letter requesting a correspondent of similar age.

How well I remembered the blustery, snowy day her letter arrived. Papa threw the mailsack down to me from atop a wagonload of hay; among the contents was a square, pink envelope with pretty, round penmanship. I couldn't have found a friend nearer my age, for her birth date and mine were exactly the same.

That evening while Papa popped corn and Mama mended, I sat by the yellow glow of the kerosene lamp in our little ranch cabin and considered interesting things I could write to Augusta. Come to think of it now, the thoughts I later put on paper must have been a bit melodramatic—coyotes howling at the starlit, winter skies—I really wanted to impress her.

Being a lone child in the country, no doubt I had more free time available than she for writing. From my wonderful Idaho in the Intermountain area of the Far West went vignettes of the lonely beauty of the sage hills, rainbow speckled minnows in the old swimming hole, purple pansy studded mesas, dashing flocks of wild birds defying description! The mild weather (no bad thunder storms) (no dangerous blizzards) (no dense fogs) (no hurricanes) (no extreme hot or cold spells) (no tornados) of the Inland Empire of the Pacific Northwest made it the finest place in the world for pie socials at the one-room school house on the hill, exciting home town rodeos, thrilling neighborhood surprise parties!

Snapshots, desert cactus, picture folders of scenes from ghost mining towns and the vast primitive areas traveled eastward, along with stories of horseback rides over the rough, Squaw Butte heights, and tales of ice jams in the raging waters of Squaw Creek in the early spring.

In self defense, Augusta enlisted the aid of her oldest sister to supervise her letters. She lovingly told about her home life in "The Land of The Sky" close to the Blue Ridge Mountains and the Great Smoky National Park. She described the brilliantly colored floats in the Rhododendron Festival; the smooth, colorful acres and acres of golf links; the pure mountain water and delightful climate which attracts thousands of tourists to Buncombe County each year. The lush-green, wooded hills of North Carolina, that turn to flaming beauty in the Southern autumn, were scenes of family drives and happy picnics with her dear mother, three older sisters, and Baptist minister father.

Into her tinted envelopes, nestled with her careful penmanship, she tucked evergreen needles, newspaper clippings, and picture post cards of thriving factories, the famous Chimney Rock, the costly and magnificent Biltmore House with its hundreds of acres of landscaped gardens, the Mountain Dance and Folk Festivals.

At first we were not aware—maybe we never were—that this was to be a friendly correspondence course in the art of correspondence. Our letters did not arrive too often, neither were they written in haste nor carelessly. Not to be outdone by the other, we each grew to be amateur word artists—constantly looking for the beautiful and unusual things with which to form pictures. This search for items of intrigue sharpened our interest in our own locales, and when we began copying some of our blessings on paper, we were suddenly acutely aware of the natural beauty in our own surroundings.

No public relations director was needed to urge us to spread friendliness between East and West, North and South. We found the real pleasures of life were increased by telling others about them. Our friends and relatives shared the letters, enjoyed the pictures. How the Chambers of Commerce would have rejoiced to have had these Ambassadors of Good Will multiplied a thousand-fold!

Throughout later years came marriage and birth announcements, gifts, photographs, tears dropped over bereavements.

Now the time had come for us to meet! In September, thirty years after the beginning of our friendship, a birthday card from Augusta came, bearing the thrilling news—"We are planning a vacation trip to the Yellowstone National Park. . . . we feel that we must come on across Idaho to see you for a few hours. . . ."

The big question: how would we appear to each other? I had not the slightest doubt about her—she would be so wonderful, so neatly dressed, talk so sweetly Southern, be so composed (how could a widow who was personnel manager of a large department store be anything else?), have her hair styled so beautifully.

But what about me? Whew! Cow-country ranch wife with no beauty treatments, no gracious living, no beautiful home to offer—well, to put it very mildly, the liabilities certainly overbalanced the assets. Also, I wondered, would my long-described, fabulous West fall short under inspection?

Still, deep within, I knew that we would never have continued thirty years of correspondence had there not been a common ground of friendship between us. There was that intangible feeling of having walked hand-in-hand together as we grew up and matured in mind.

A weather report on the radio bore the alarming news: the first snow storm of the season was bearing down on the Rockies. Bad luck! What if they grew frightened of the snow in our mountains and turned back before getting to Idaho. When I figured the day had arrived, I decided to stay dressed in my jeans—there being a shadow of superstition in my mind that if I put on dress, slippers, and nylons, they wouldn't arrive.

But at four o'clock, down the driveway they came! Gus was a better runner than I; she met me with open arms before I reached the gate—more beautiful, more young looking, more overflowing with force and vitality than I had imagined! Friends united! Our love for each other was infectious, spreading to other involved members of our families; even the wary, little cattle dog that sometimes tried to nip strangers came right up to be petted by a friend.

The weekend couldn't provide enough day or night hours for all of our radiant conversation. We hadn't thought of having physical resemblances, but there they were—a surprise! We really didn't look alike, yet our hands were small and of the same shape; our eyes light-and-far sensitive and a like shade of blue. Our hair was brown and cut short. Our weight varied little. Our heights were identical—five foot one. Neither or us used tobacco nor profanity. We both enjoyed the same kinds of foods.

But what was far more important, our opinions, sympathies, faiths, views, inner qualities of mind were so very similar.

It was a sad parting. When the hour came for Gus to leave on her 2,700 mile journey home, we hardly dared look at each other. We blinked back the tears through our smiles and good-wishes, for well we knew that we might never meet again.

With blurred eyes I watched the last of the dust on the driveway. Now that Gus had come and gone, I had time to sit and ponder. . . . Why were we so much alike? Was it because we were born on the same day, under Virgo, or could it have been because her maiden name was Corn, and my maiden name was Bean?

November 5 *Squash Ethics*

After the arrival of the garden tractor, I decided to go ahead with the little squash business that Dan had started and built up as a 4-H project.

We have several regular customers who watch for our squash sign to be put up each fall of the year. Many say that they have been disappointed with squashes they have purchased down in the valley—they were pale colored, or watery, or stringy, or lacked sugar, or were flavorless. A person never knows how a squash will taste until it is cooked, as each has its own, individual flavor. However, the larger percentage of ours have been of excellent quality; whether it is the variety, soil, climate, or irrigating methods, I do not know.

Hunters are usually good customers, especially if they have had poor luck in hunting—they don't like to go home empty handed. It also gives them an excuse to stop to nonchalantly inquire about hunting conditions.

I have learned many certain facts in the squash business; one is: never underestimate the buying power of any person. A big car full of men may drive in. You think, "Boy, oh, boy, here's where I sell a lot of squashes," but, in all probability, they will purchase only one small one. On the other hand, a little old widow, who you know can't eat very much, may linger until she selects over a hundred pounds. One customer, a woman who runs her own cattle ranch, buys three hundred pounds each fall to give away to friends and relatives. Others buy a year's supply to store away in the freezer or can.

Last week a white-haired man, with his wife and tiny dog, drove out from Boise in his old jalopy and bought two of the largest orange banana squash. Yesterday they returned with a trailer bumping along behind. When I met him at the gate, I remarked, "You must have liked that squash."

He answered, "Say, that was the best squash I ever tasted in all my life. I went down to the super-market where we trade and told them that they should buy all of these good squashes. The manager said, 'That's what we want—good squashes. I'll take 800 pounds of big ones if you'll bring them in to me.' So I have brought my trailer to get them. He will send you the money."

Added his wife, "We just couldn't stand to think about those delicious squashes lying out there in that shed until they froze."

I was trying to think fast. This was a strange deal. Should I let a total stranger haul away a whole load of squash without a cent of payment? The man looked honest, but a person couldn't always tell by that. I remembered reading in a farm magazine that ninety-some per cent of all customers were honest. I decided to take the chance.

We weighed and carried out all of the large orange bananas, and had to fill in with smaller blue ones. His trailer would hold only 600 pounds.

When Clark learned that the man's trailer hitch had broken on the way over, he hunted another old one in the shop and welded it on. As they pulled out of the driveway, Clark and I laughed and wondered if we would ever see the money.

Today, the very next day, the check came in the mail!

That good old Missourian had gone to the trouble of making the sale to the store, and had driven one-hundred miles to get and deliver the squashes, without expecting or accepting a dime for his services. I could understand why he was driving such an old car—all of his life he had been giving to others—a fine, generous, unselfish person.

November 17 Well, Well

Five hundred dollars, that is what it will cost by the time we get it all paid for, the well drilling, the deep well pump, the pipes, the housing to cover it. A lot of money to pay for pure drinking water, yet how can a family conveniently get along without it?

We have been hauling our drinking water in a ten gallon milk can for over a year, ever since we had our old well water tested and found it to be contaminated. I certainly can sympathize with early settlers out on the deserts who had to haul all of their water in barrels on a wagon for many miles.

This part of the country is blessed with hundreds of springs, but they aren't always situated handy to the farmsteads.

We are hoping the new well will furnish enough water for a lawn. It is located below the house in a desolate spot—I say "desolate" because our once beautiful cherry trees stand dead or dying beside it. The autumn freeze of 1955 is gradually killing them limb by limb. We can't boast of our fruit growing record: First our young peach orchard winterkilled. We set out a new long row of peach seedlings and budded onto them—they all winterkilled the very first winter! The boys helped me dig holes for setting eight grape vines (Concords, the hardy variety)—and all died but one, and it freezes back each spring. The pear trees had to be pulled, then the diseased black raspberries. I tried planting a sour cherry tree, bush cherry, and black walnuts, but they just wouldn't live, even after months of care and water.

December 6 Last Pig

We sold our last pig today. That means we are going out of the hog business for now at least. Ever since the leptospirosis invaded our herd, the litters have been too small to pay their way.

We had put so much effort, time, and money into developing a profitable breeding line; and they were such sleek, trim, prize winning stock, that we were reluctant to see them go. Perhaps if the hog market didn't drop so often, and Clark didn't have to work away from home, we could have gone into a tedious vaccinating routine that might have saved more pigs. However, it takes several years and considerable advertising to build up a breeding-stock market, which is quickly shattered by an insidious disease of this and other kinds. One year our market was ruined by a crippling attack of erysipelas, just before a safe vaccine was developed.

Anyway, the riddance of hogs will eliminate some of the daily chores, and my troubles of keeping the garden fence hog tight and of having irrigation ditches rooted or wallowed out.

December 30 Going—Going—Gone

Our purpose in moving back to the ranch—to allow the boys to grow up in a more wholesome atmosphere or environment—has nearly been accomplished.

John and Dan have been working summers in woods or construction jobs and are majoring in forestry at the University of Idaho—John in his third year, Dan in his first. Jim, a high school senior this year, is planning on going east to study electronics next fall.

As in the case of many other ranchers, whose land will not support a family and who are working part time off the farm to supplement their incomes, Clark is also working, but not part time. He is working steady on the night shift at a sawmill twenty-five miles away down in the valley. At 3:15 a.m., in the coldest part of the morning when he returns home from work, he starts up the tractor and hauls hay to the range cattle, and hauls some more in the afternoon before returning to work. Jim feeds and milks the dairy cows before and after bus and school hours.

Although we are cutting down on chores by gradually selling the dairy cows and hogs, we will no longer have enough help to run the ranch. Summertime work of keeping up fences, managing the beef cattle, planting and harvesting the crops, and maintaining the equipment is more work than one man can do full time. At the present level of farm commodity prices, this place will not support us, let alone a hired man. Since none of the boys are studying agriculture, it is unlikely that they will care to return to the ranch to live, or find it economically feasible.

Obviously, sooner or later, changes on the ranch are going to have to be made.

— 1988 —
EPILOGUE

The boys went on to higher learning—John graduated from the University of Idaho in 1959 with a bachelor's degree in the Science of Forestry. He served six years in the National Guard. After graduation, he accepted a position with the State of Oregon Department of Revenue, Timber Severance Tax Section, Assessment and Appraisal Division, and is now East Oregon Region Manager.

Dan also studied forestry for two years at the University of Idaho, then worked in the timber and wood products industry, and was a maintenance supervisor for a Boise Cascade plywood plant. He also served six years in the Idaho National Guard, two years on active duty. He now owns and operates a jersey dairy farm in the Emmett, Idaho, Valley.

In 1959, Jim went to Chicago and received a diploma upon completion of a 36-week residential training program in Controls for Automation, from DeVry Technical Institute. Then he attended Oregon Technical Institute in Klamath Falls, Oregon, and received an associate degree in Electronics Technology. He worked for the Boeing Company in Seattle and Ford Philco in California before finally settling down in the Timber and Woods Products Department of Boise Cascade Corporation. At the present time he is studmill superintendent of the Elgin, Oregon, Complex. He is chairman of the State of Oregon Industrial Electrical Apprenticeship Committee, and has been a member of the local city council and school board.

All of the boys are married, have grown children and some grandchildren.

After the boys left home for college, or careers of their own, we could no longer do all the farm work, so we moved onto a small farm down in the Emmett Valley, where the land could be leased out, and Clark wouldn't have so far to drive to work at the sawmill. Also, on his vacations, we could travel around the West in our travel trailer (without worrying about cattle and crops). Clark fished and gathered oysters on the Pacific Coast, while I formed driftwood art for gift shops, and wrote articles for travel magazines. We even drove back to North Carolina to visit my pen pal, Gus.

We allowed an older couple with their son and daughter-in-law to move into our ranch house on Squaw Creek.

One day my brother Everett, who lived north of Sweet, telephoned to tell us that a fire was raging up at our ranch. We jumped into the car (with wet burlap sacks) and drove the 35 miles. But when we arrived, all the buildings and trees were burning—no way could we save anything. The old-fashioned cook stove and many other antiques were gone. A fire of unknown origin had swept up around the bend in the creek toward the buildings. The men renters had gone fishing, and the women were so scared they jumped into their car and raced away.

Later we sold the ranch to another cattleman who uses all the ground for cattle grazing.

Around 1970, I decided to get all the scraps of paper together on which I had written a few ranch happenings when I had time (thank goodness I hadn't left them to get burned up) and compose an organized log book—sort of a sequel to a letter of mine that *Reader's Digest* had printed before we moved to the ranch so long ago—in it I had given nostalgic reasons we were taking the boys back to the farm. So many readers had written nice letters to me, complimenting our decision, I thought they might like to know how the venture turned out.

Now we stay on our farm in the Emmett Valley during the summer months, and our winters in Yuma, Arizona, where we have a mobile home. Because of Clark's ill health, we no longer take side trips. He teaches a class how to cut and polish pretty stones, a lapidary skill, once a week at the Yuma Adult Center. If I have any leisure time, I read, write, sew, or do fancy needlework.

Colophon

This first edition of *Life in the Upper Country* appears in two versions totalling 500 copies. Both versions have text set in Globe Gothic and Carmine Tango; one version (450 copies) is perfect bound. The other version (50 copies) is a limited, casebound, signed & numbered artist's book, half of which is sold as part of the Centennial Edition of *cold-drill Magazine.*

In addition to the standard text, the second version contains an inset, pressed specimen of Evelyn Amos' favorite flower, lupine, collected in the summer of 1989 (with the assistance of Tara Burt) from the site of the old Amos homestead. This version also includes a lace snowflake (crocheted for the diary by Kay E. Collins), black & white photos (courtesy of the Amos family, & Charles Scheer & the Photography Department at Simplot-Micron Technology Center, BSU), & facsimile pages of Kraft paper bags, old envelopes & bulk mailers on which Mrs. Amos kept her original diary. This version was bound by Alfred Bond of the Eagle Hand Bindery in Eagle, Idaho, & has been signed by its author, designers/editors, & binder.

Both versions have been word processed by Darla Rankin & Debi Koski of the BSU Department of English. The BSU Printing & Graphics Center is responsible for phototypesetting (Dana Robinson on the Compugraphic 8400 phototypesetter), pasteup & design (Chris Latter), & printing (Ellie Hill on a Hamada 612 press). Additional printing by Thomson-Shore of Dexter, Michigan. Inks are PMS process black & green (#5555) on Kraft index, and #60 pound Natural Text, acid-free paper.

Tom Trusky   Kay E. Collins   Will Spearman

Designers & Editors

Alfred Bond

Binder

1	2	3	4	5	6	7	8	9	10
11	12	13	14	15	16	17	18	19	20
21	22	23	24	25	26	27	28	29	30
31	32	33	34	35	36	37	38	39	40
41	42	43	44	45	46	47	48	49	50